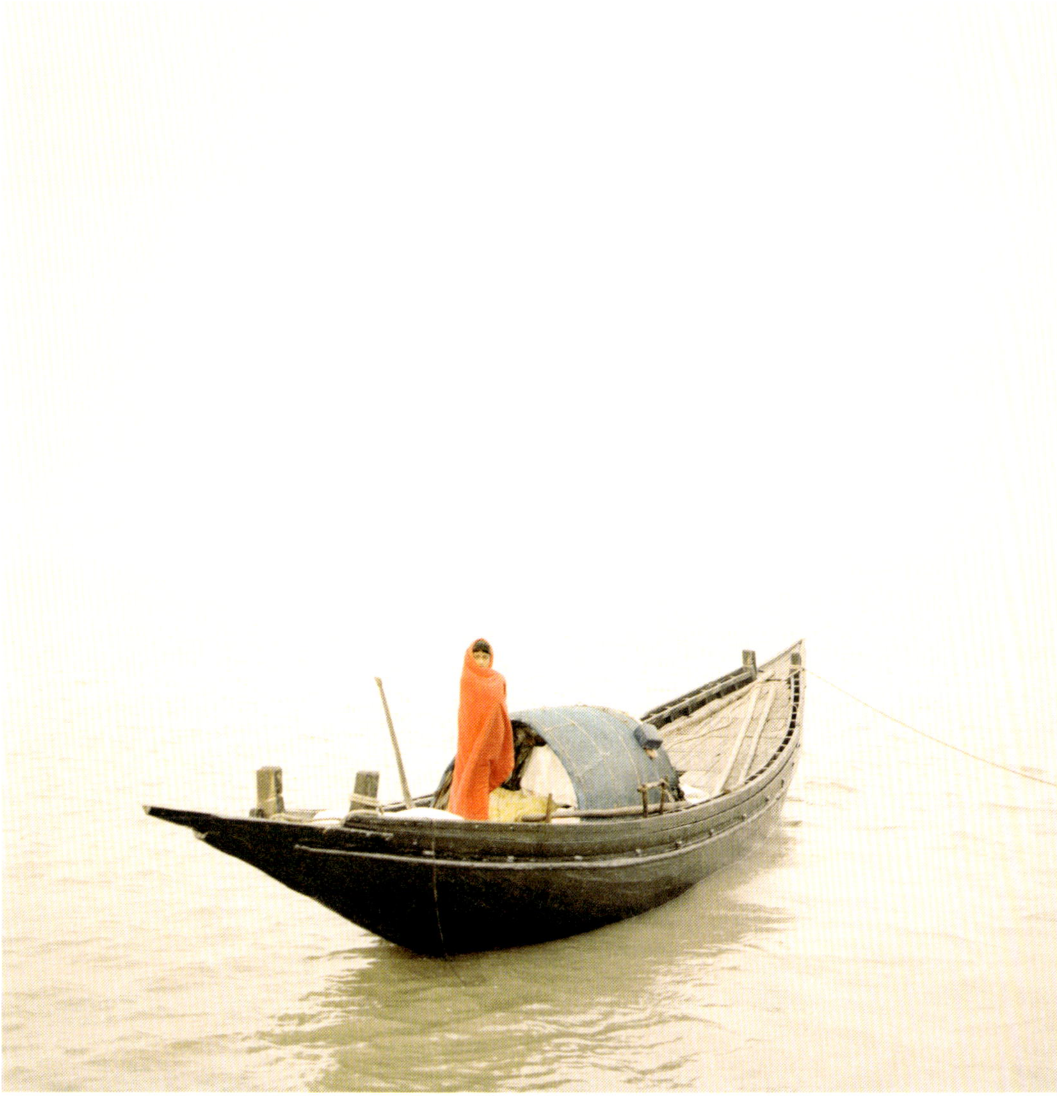

Giulio Di Sturco

Ganga Ma

GOST

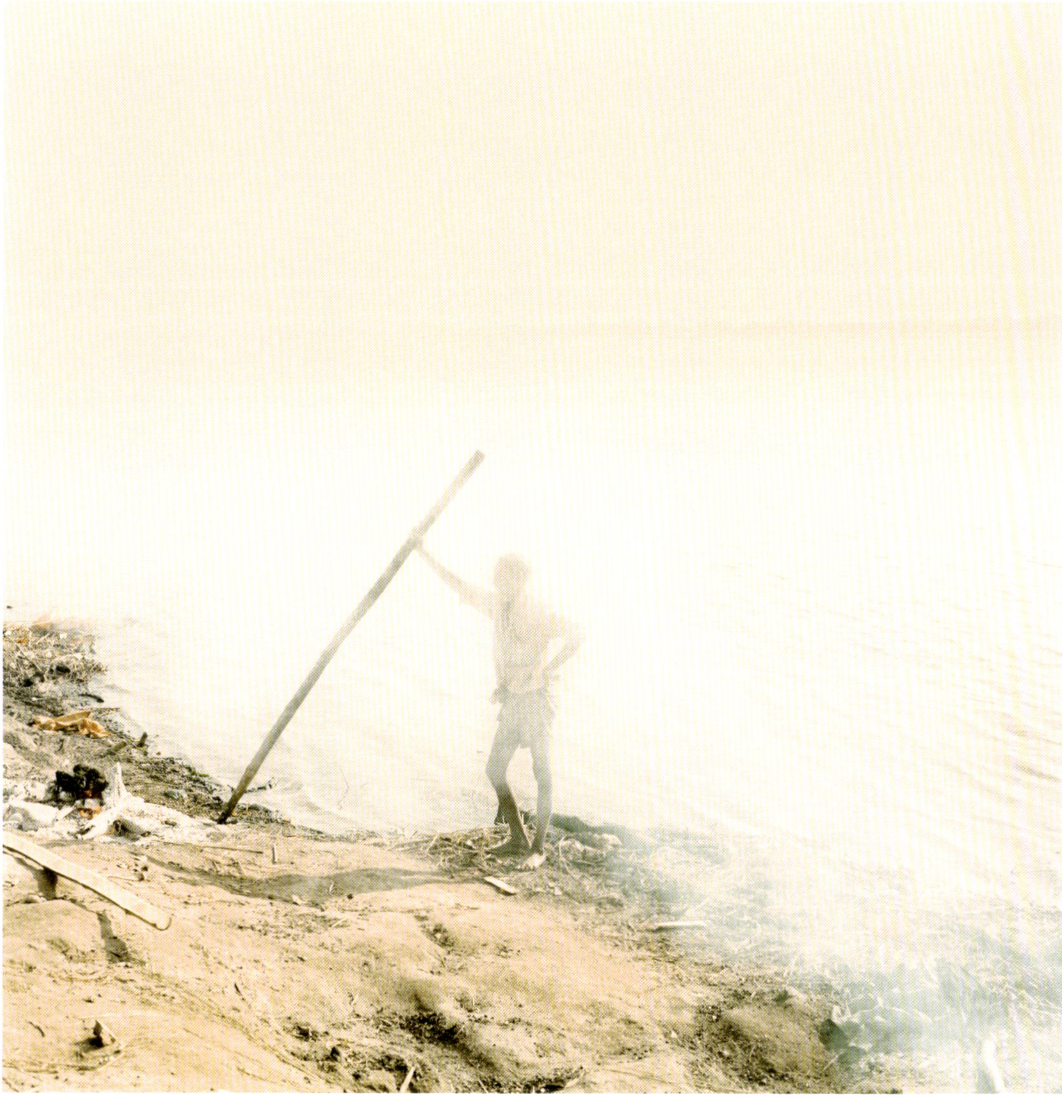

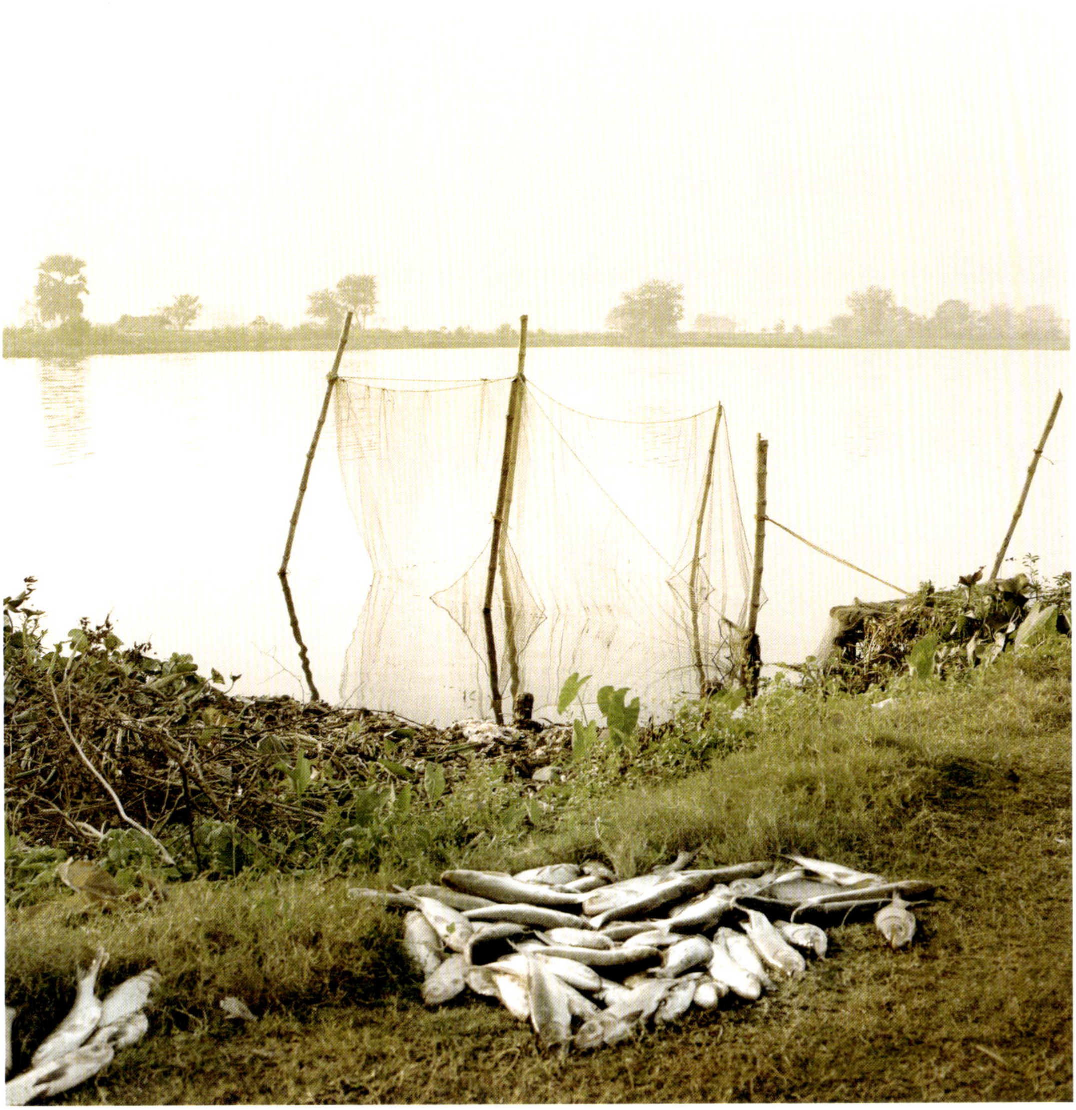

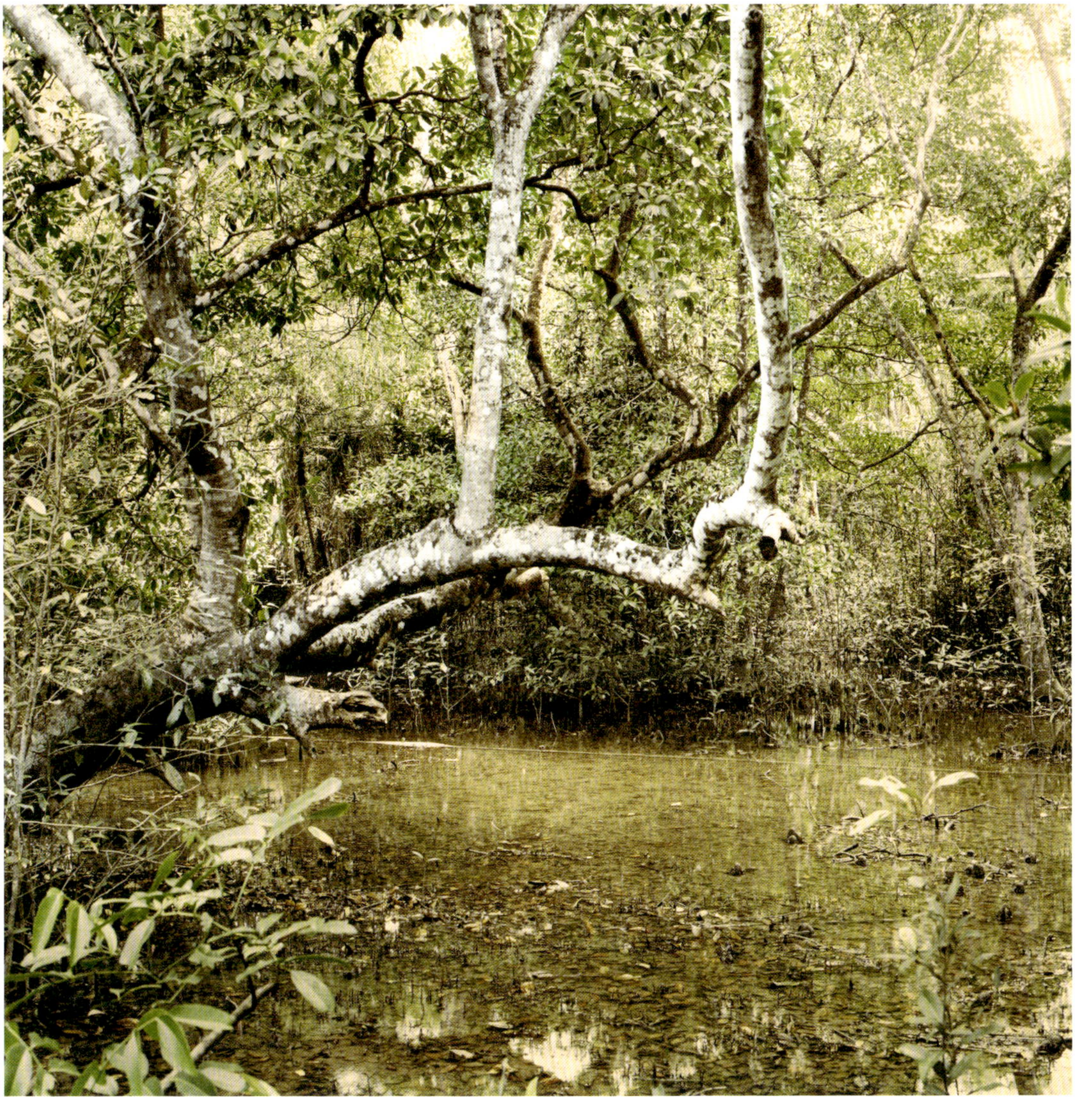

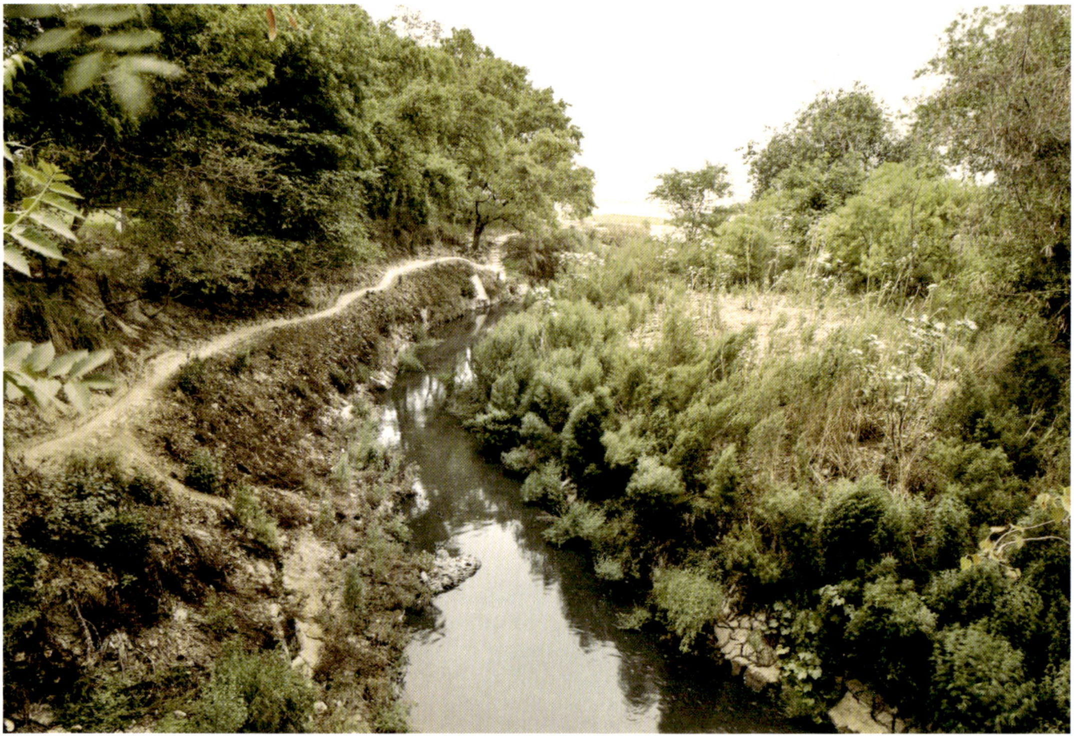

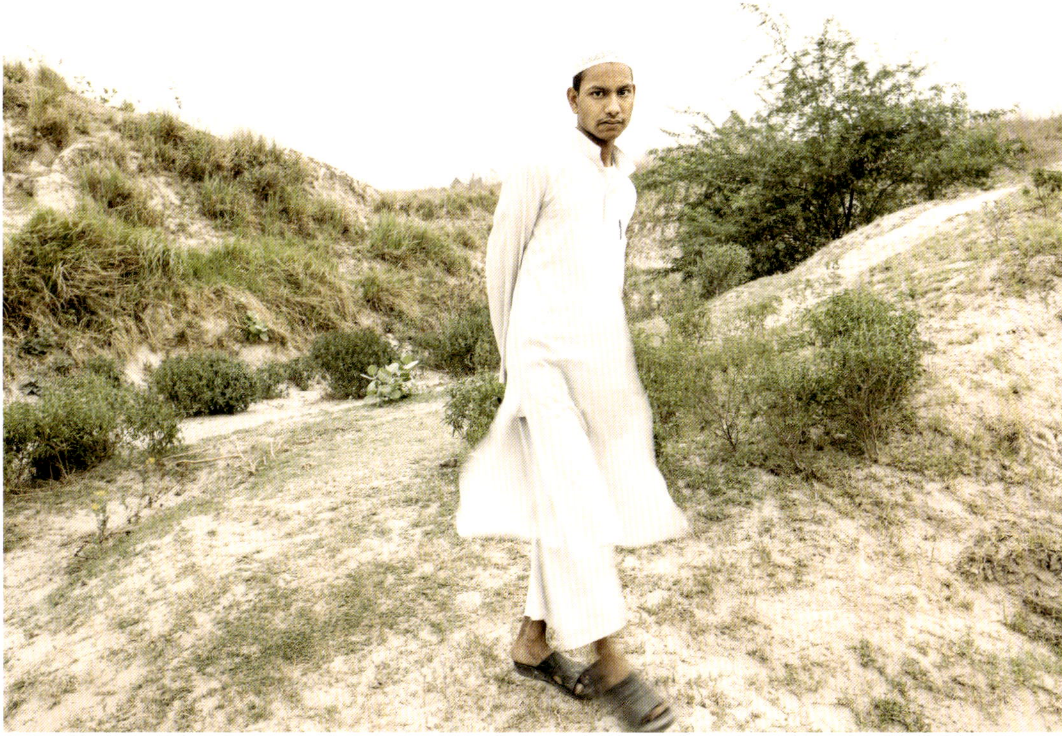

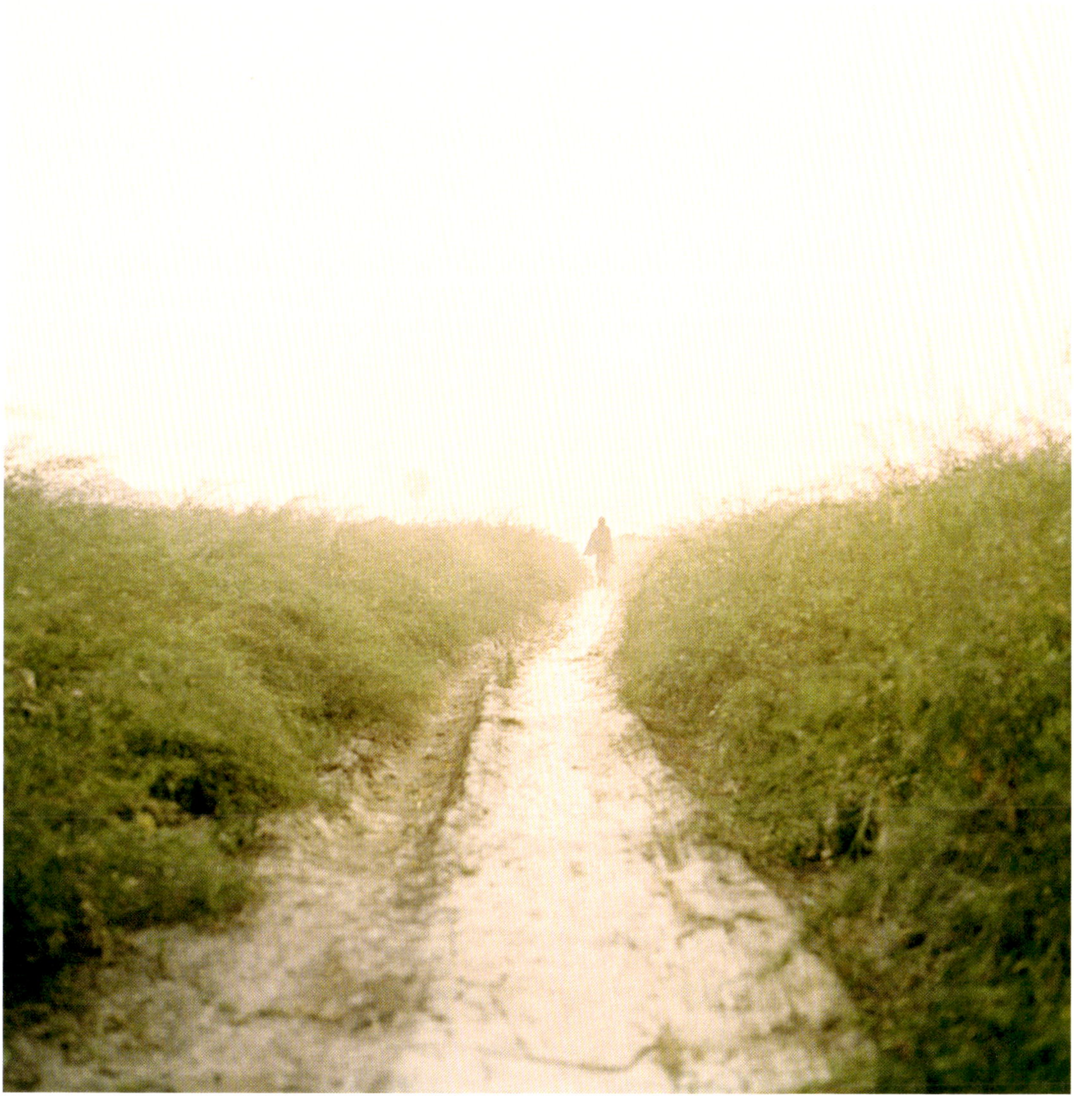

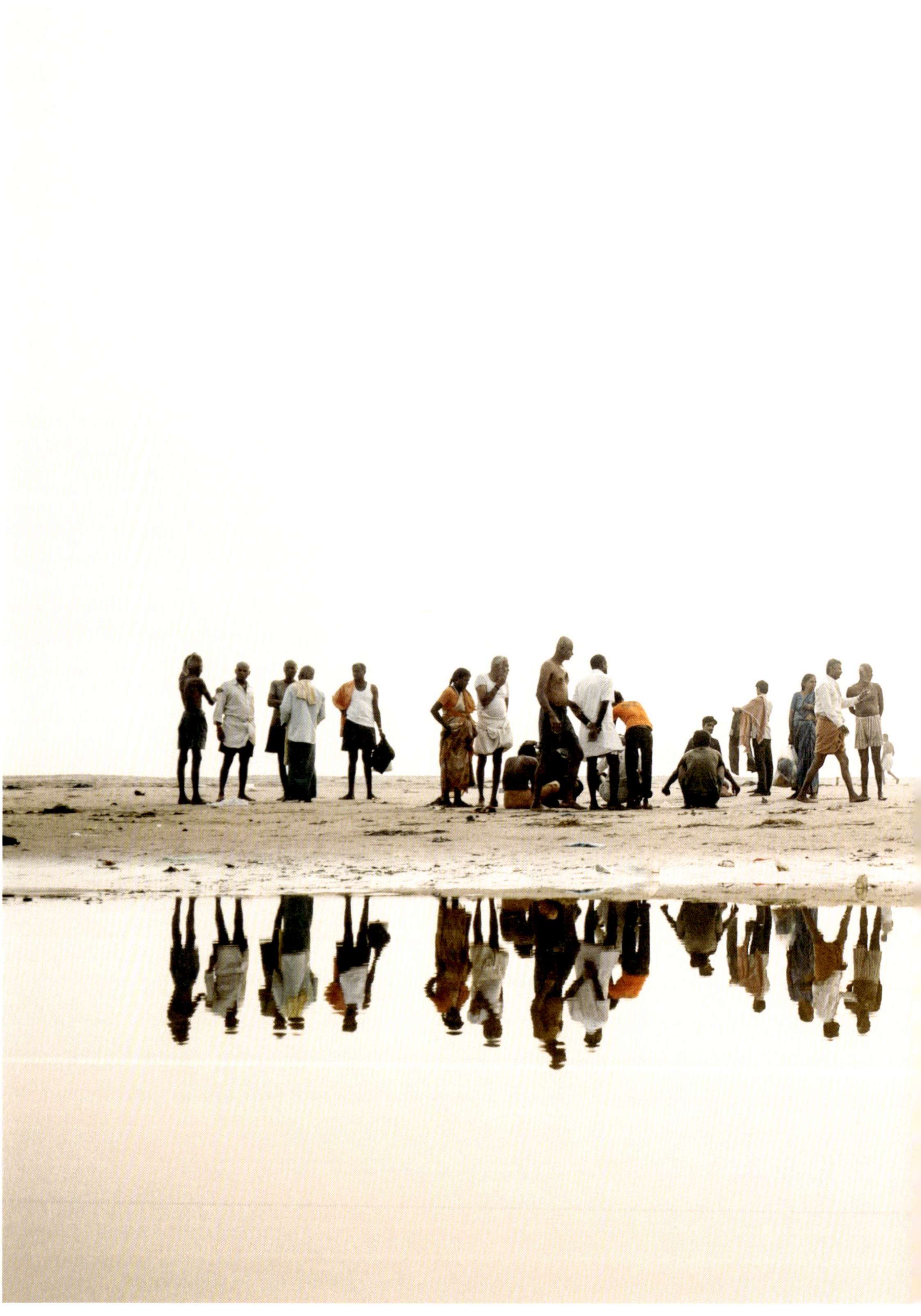

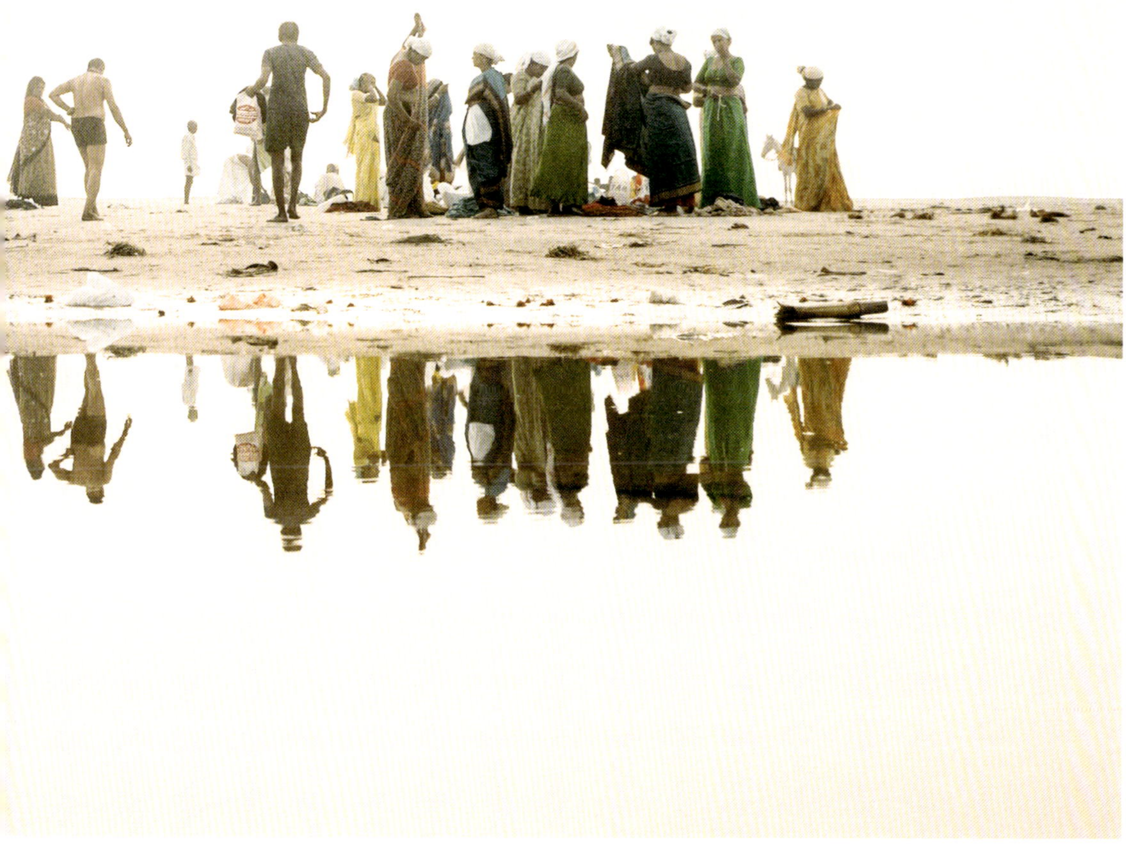

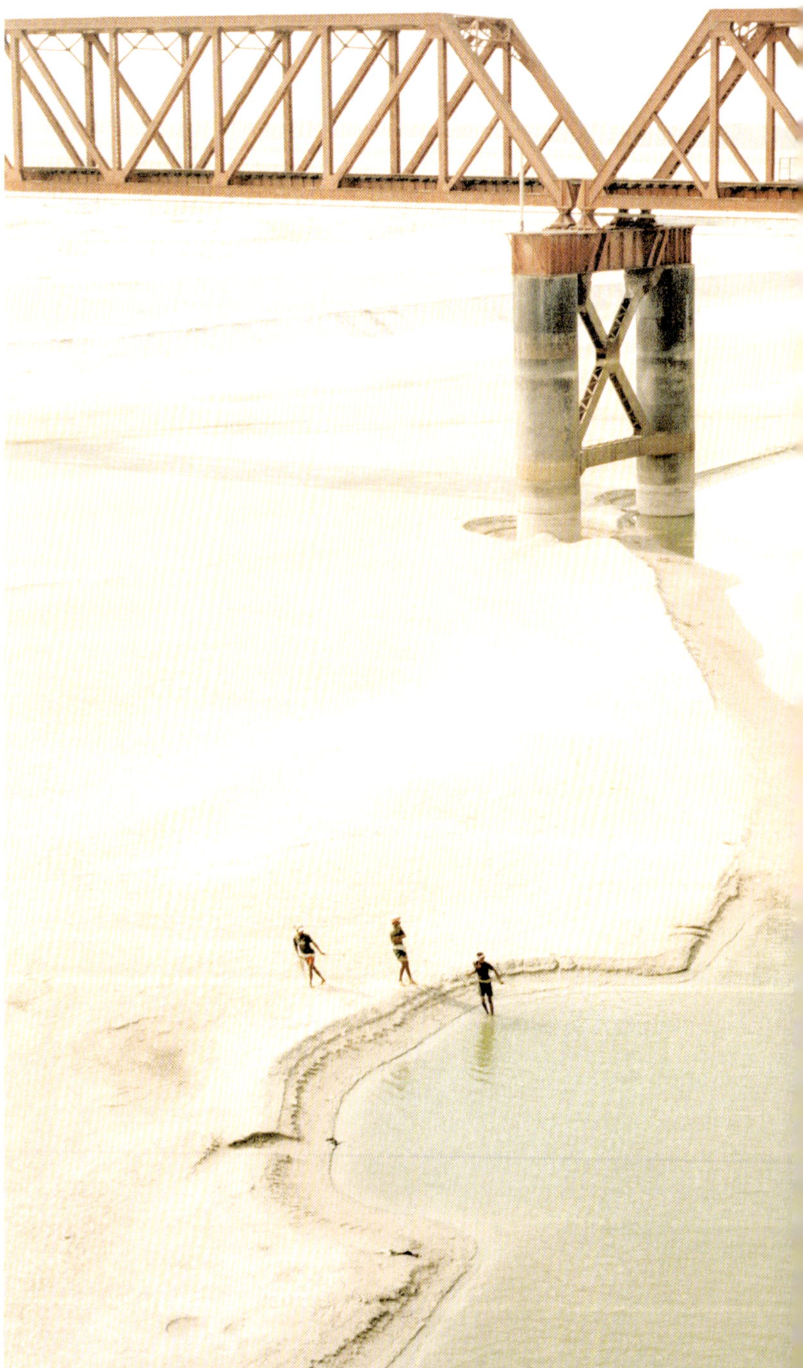

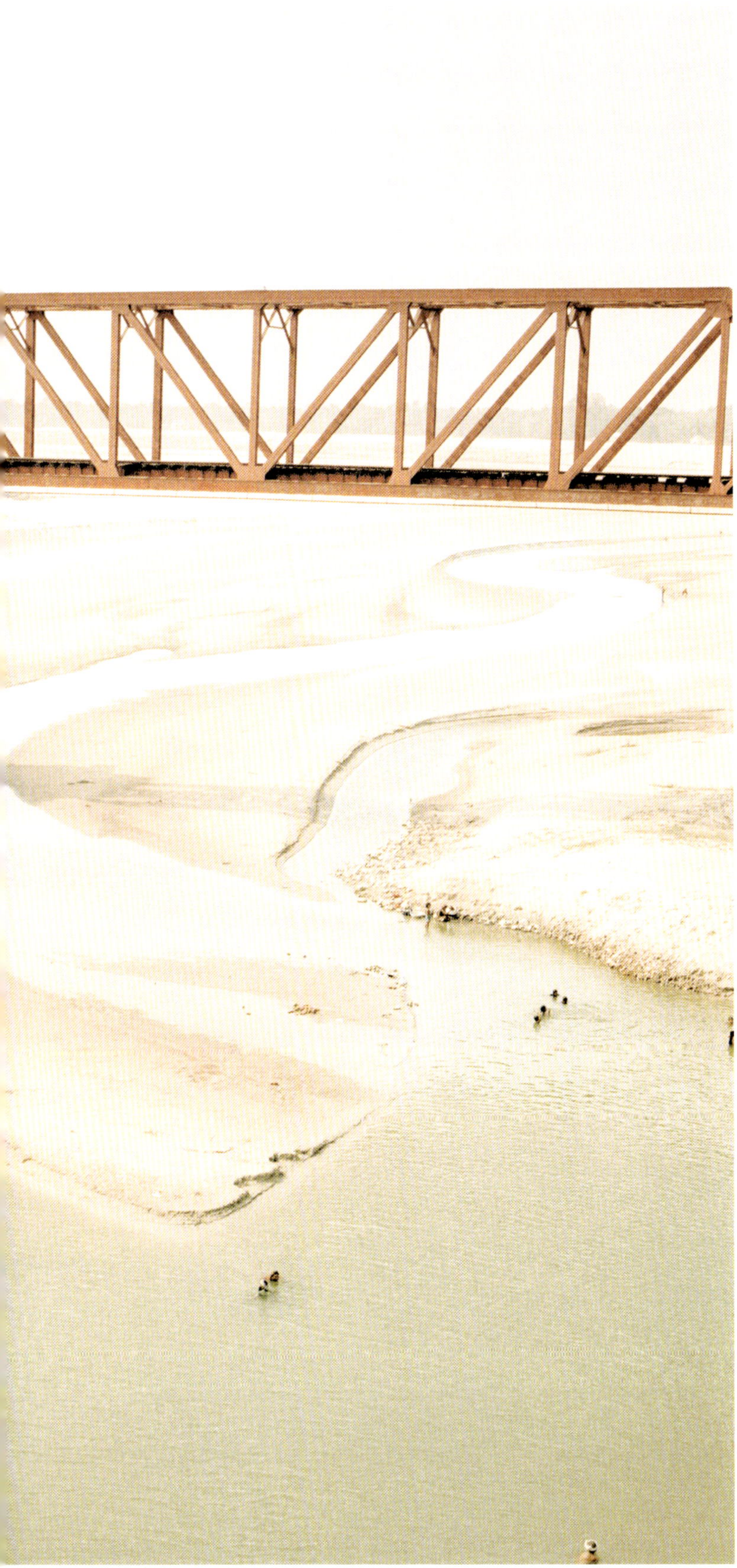

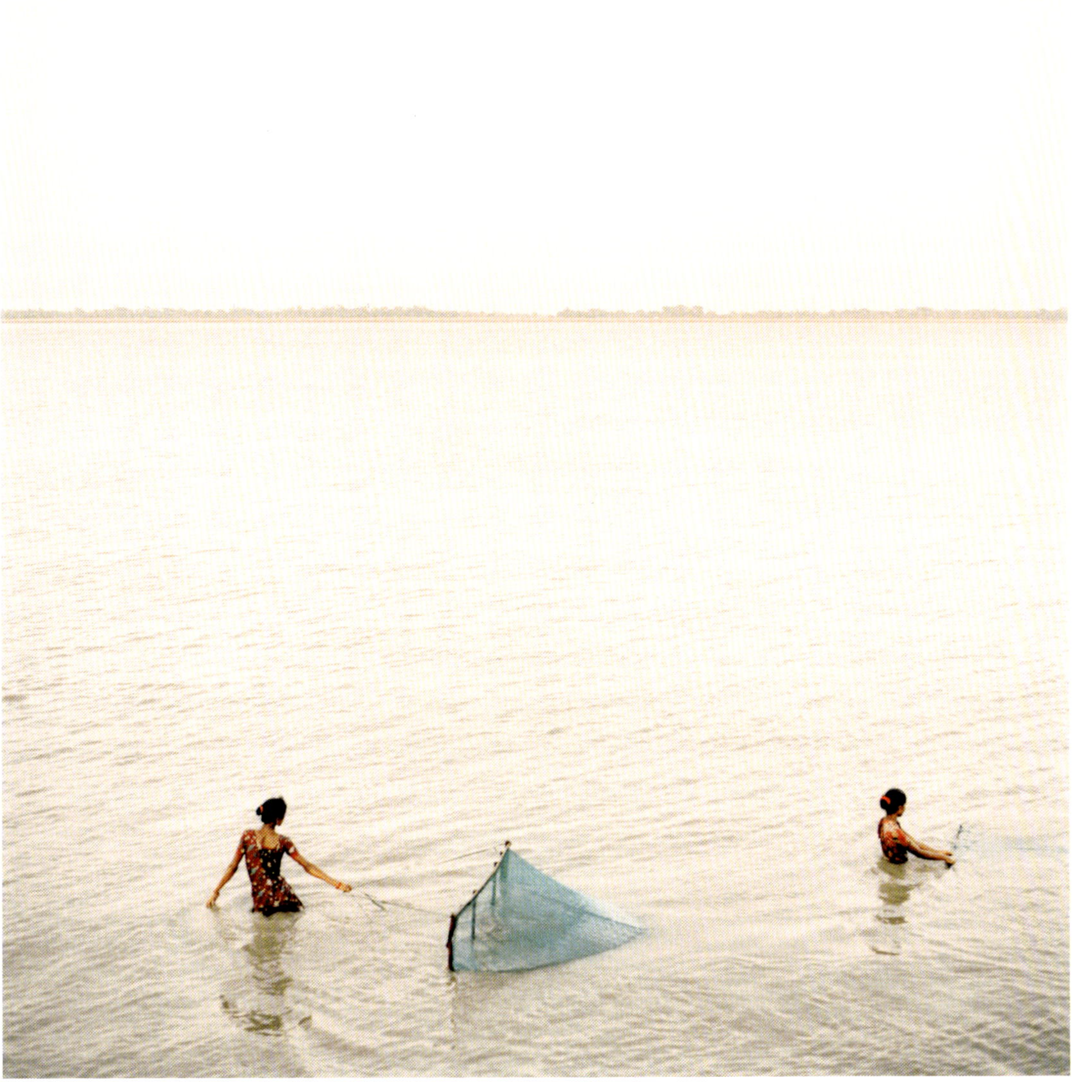

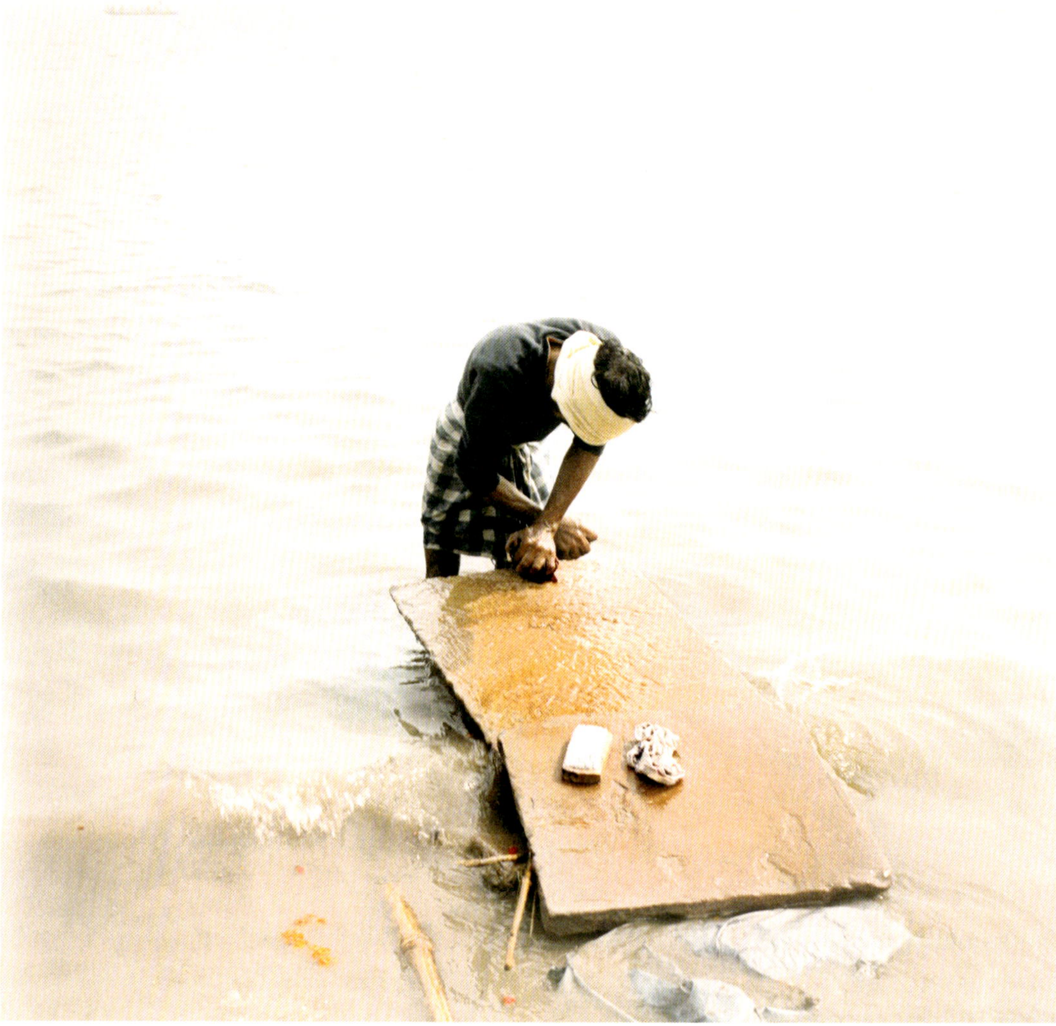

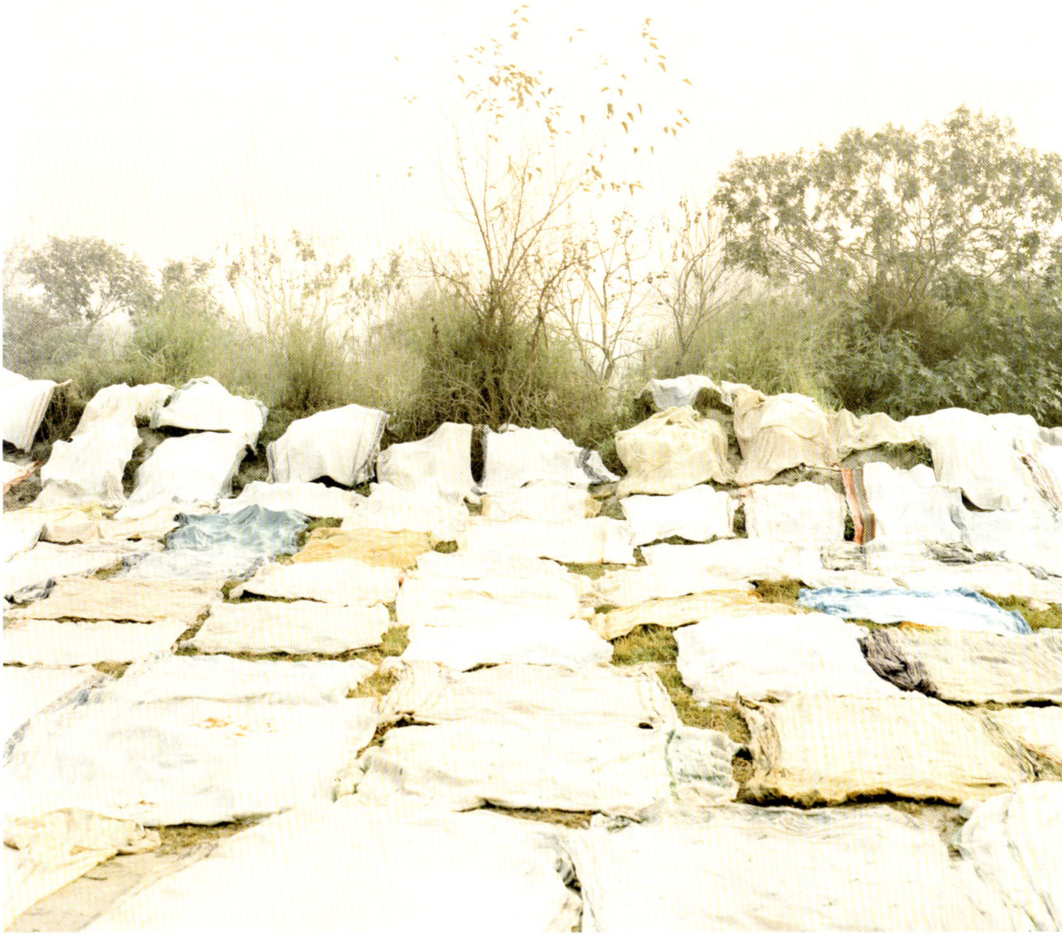

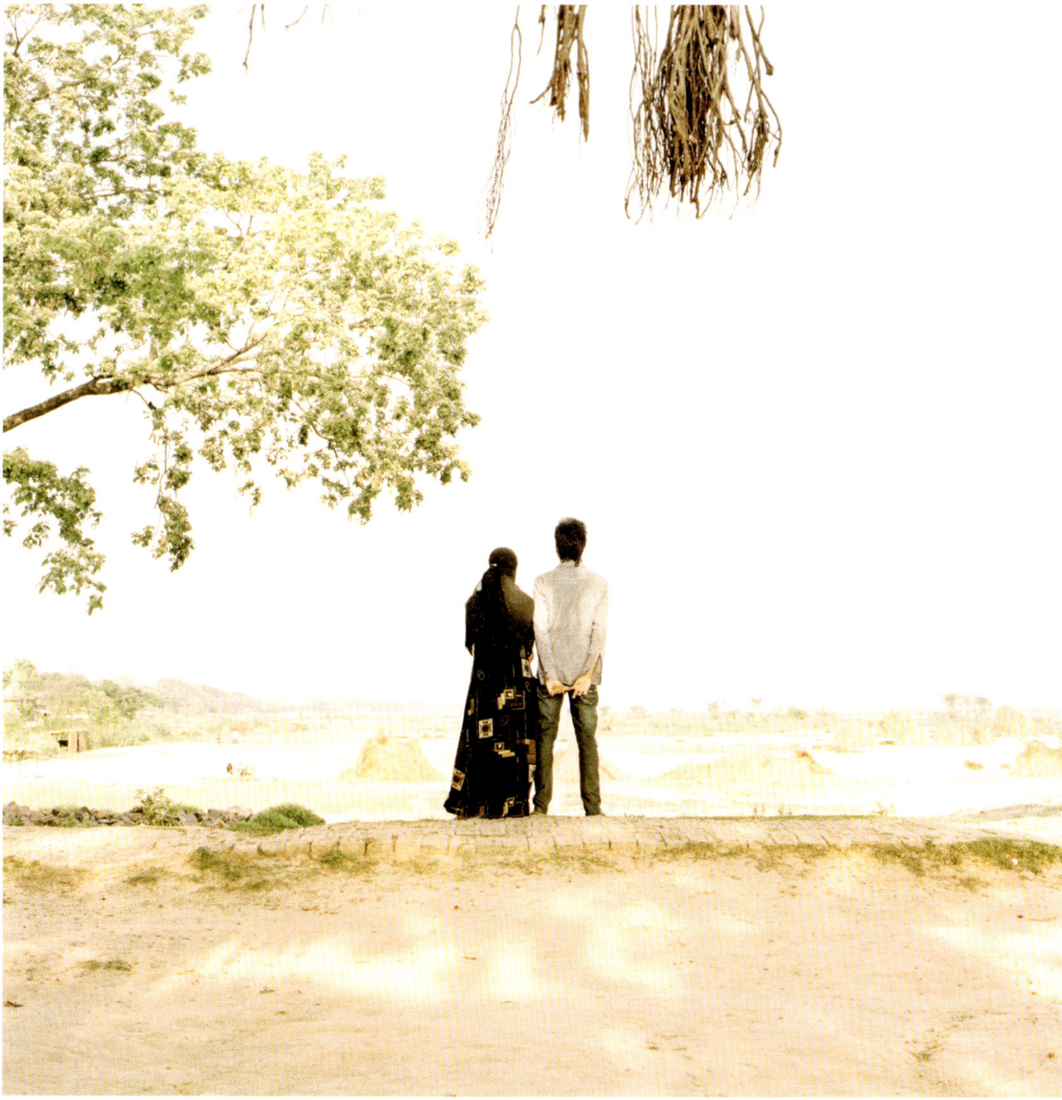

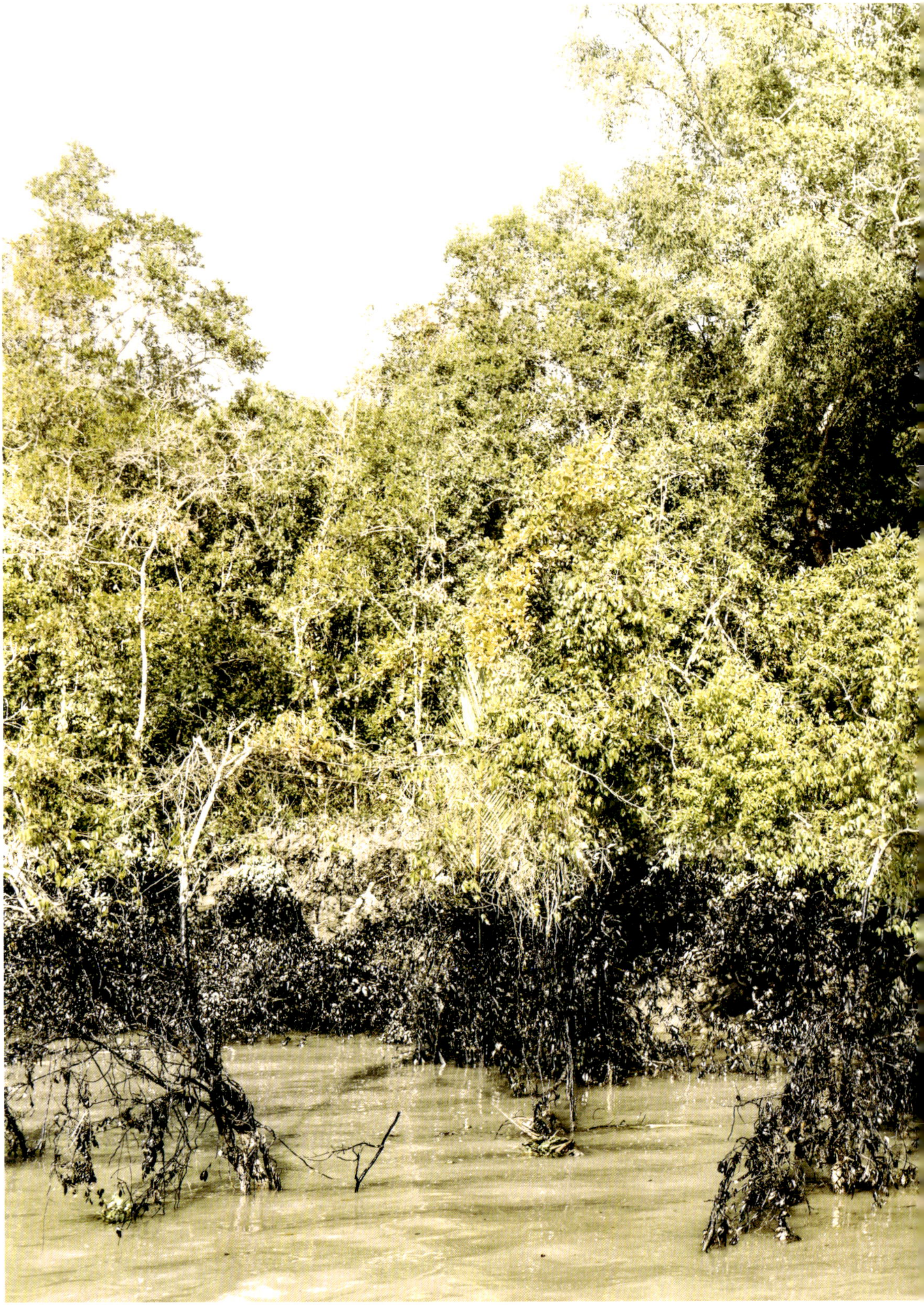

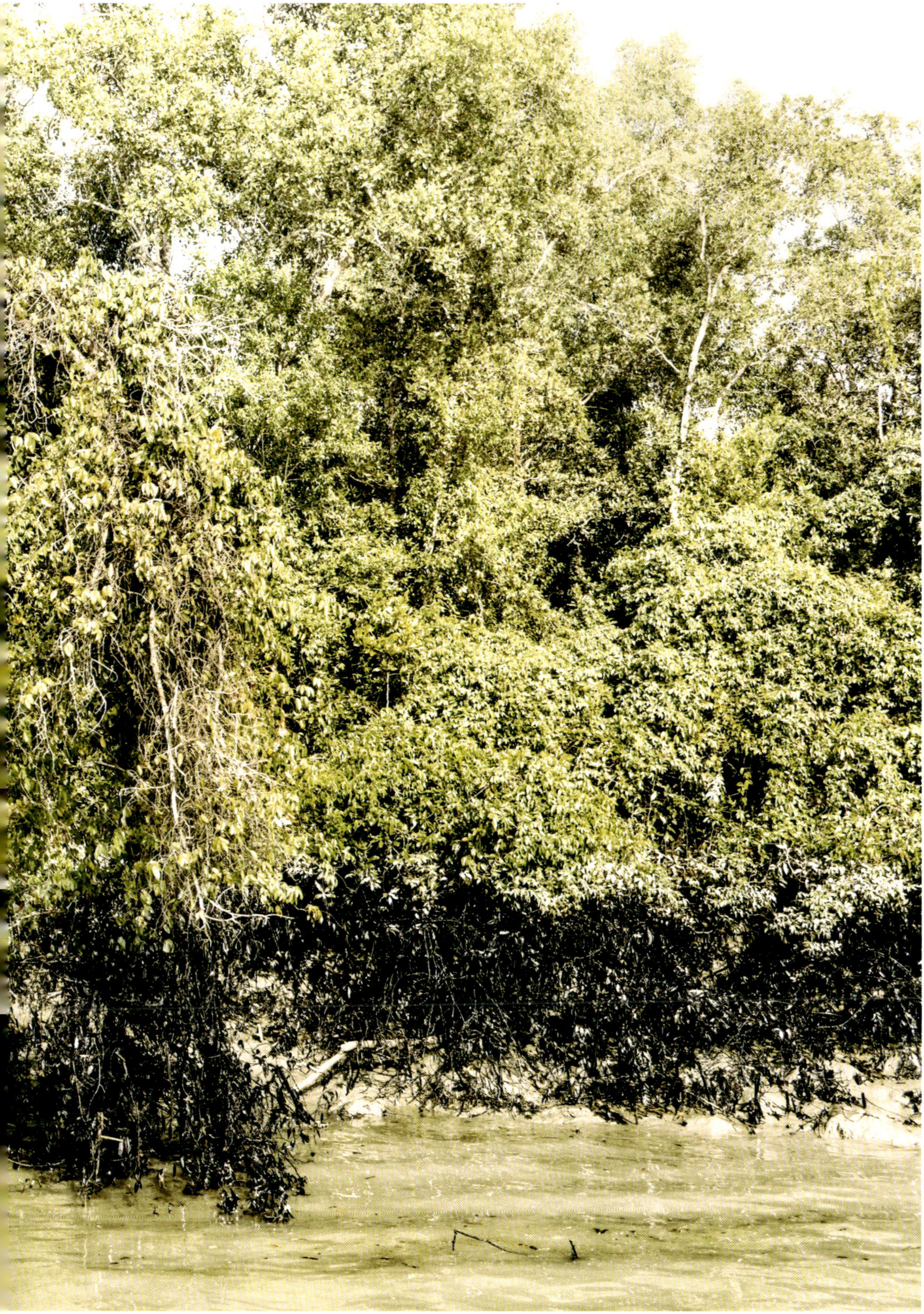

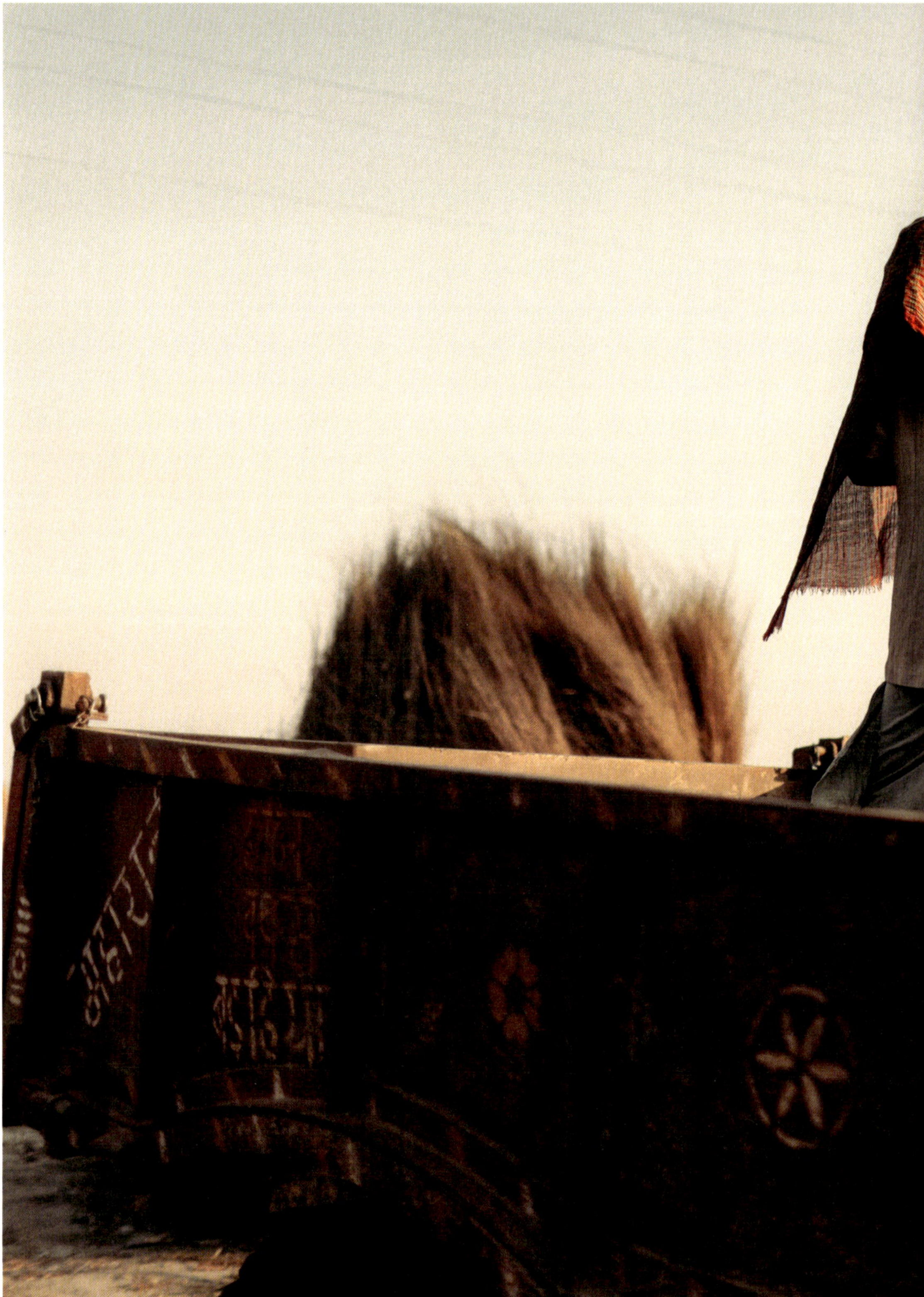

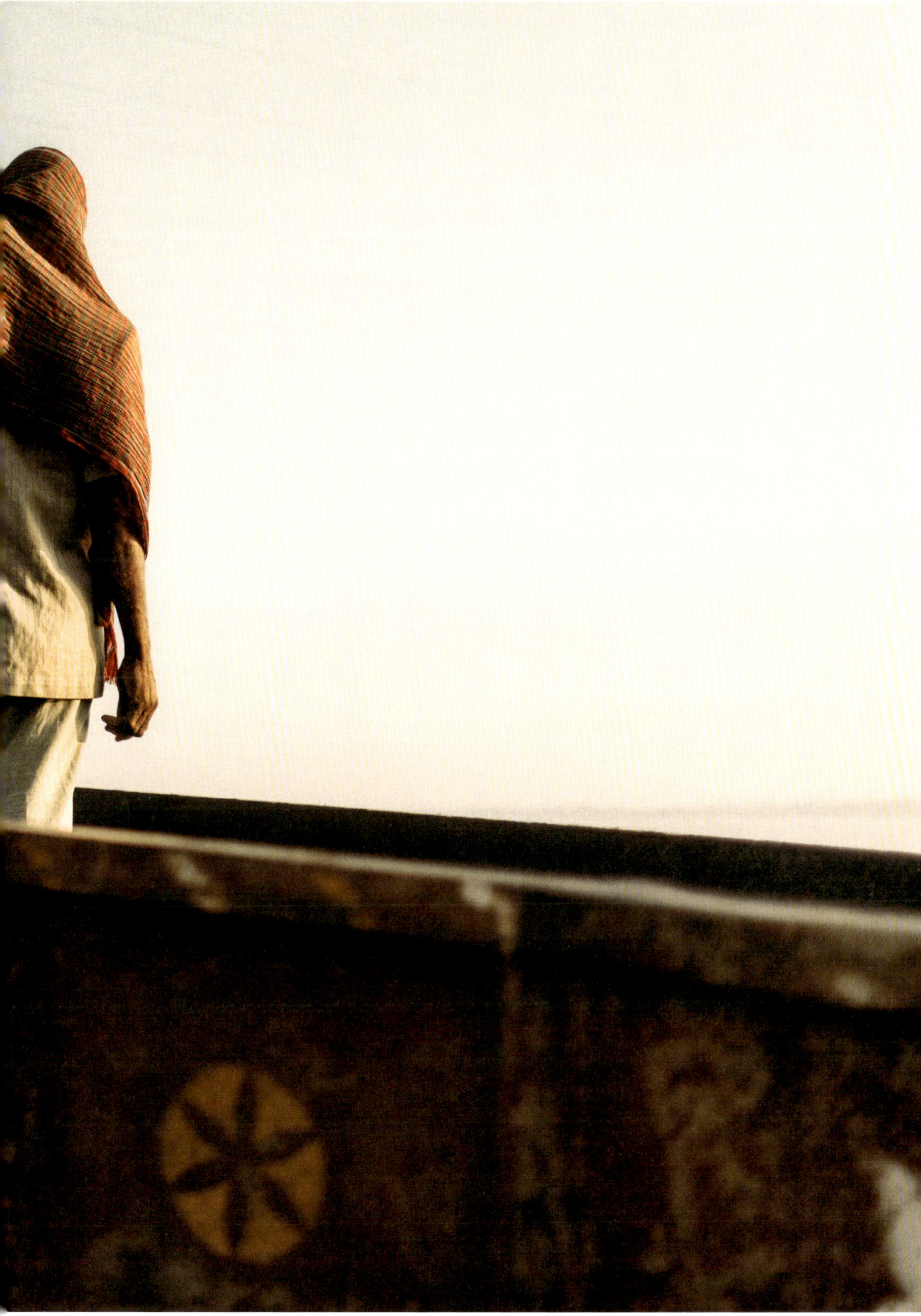

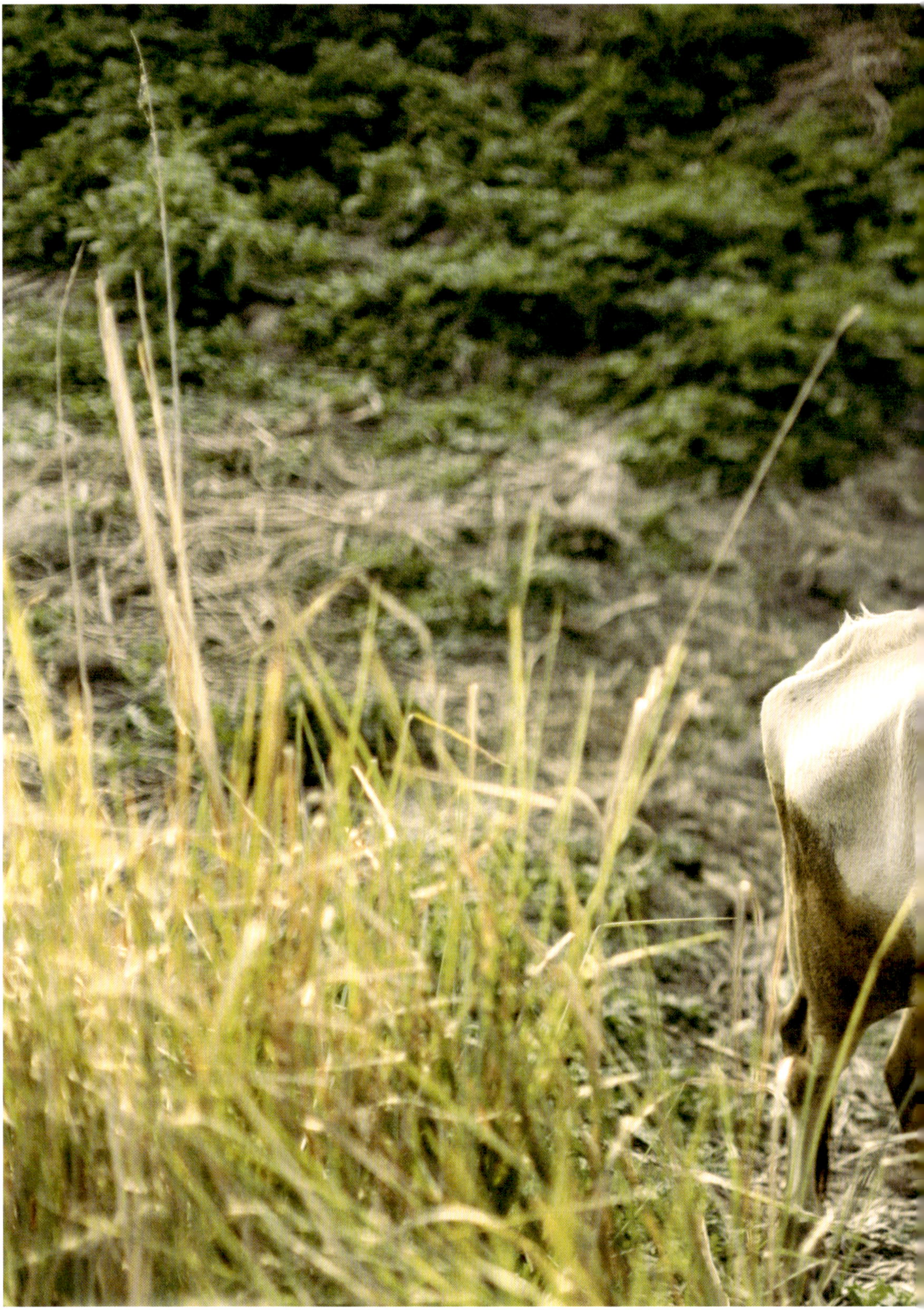

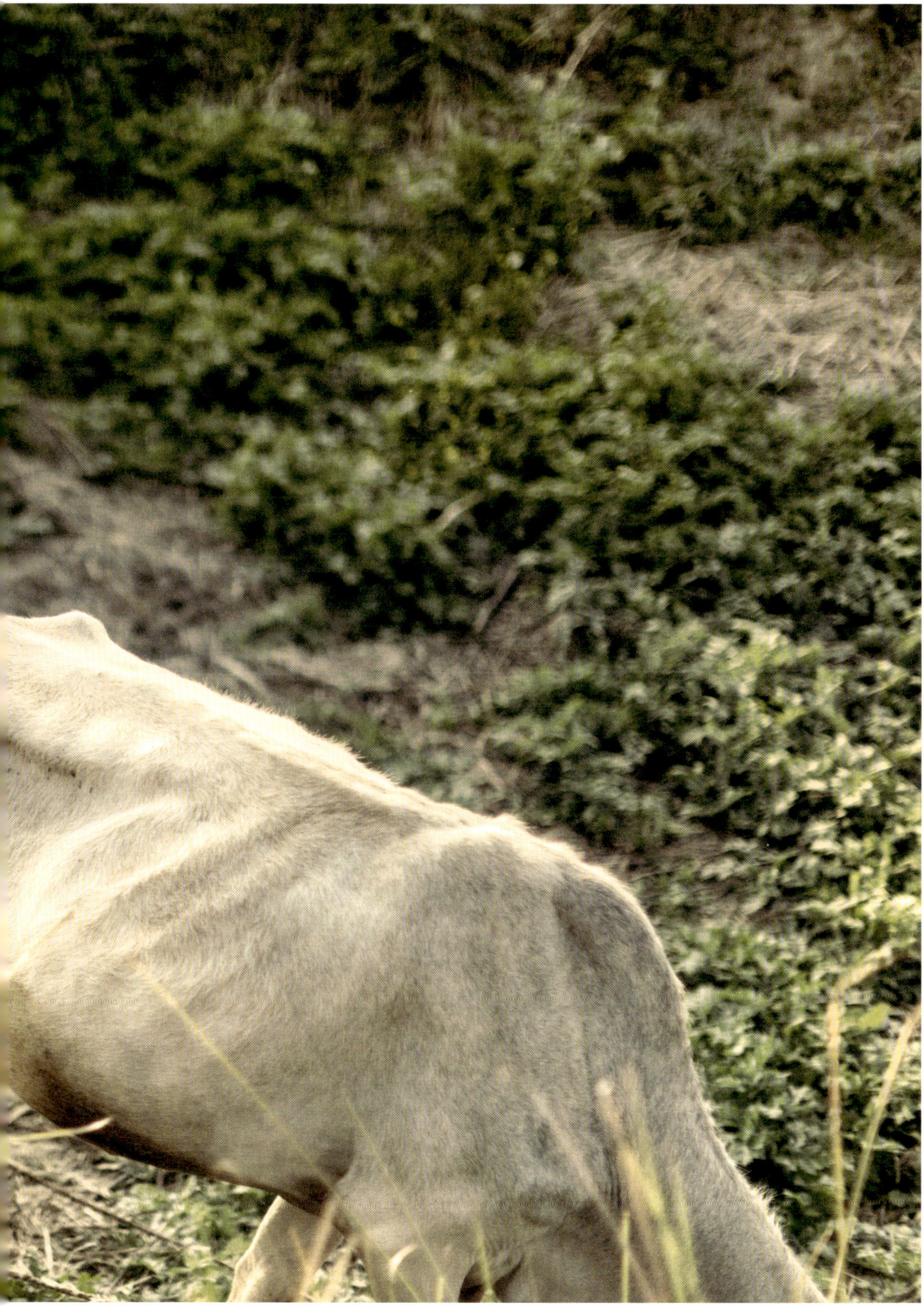

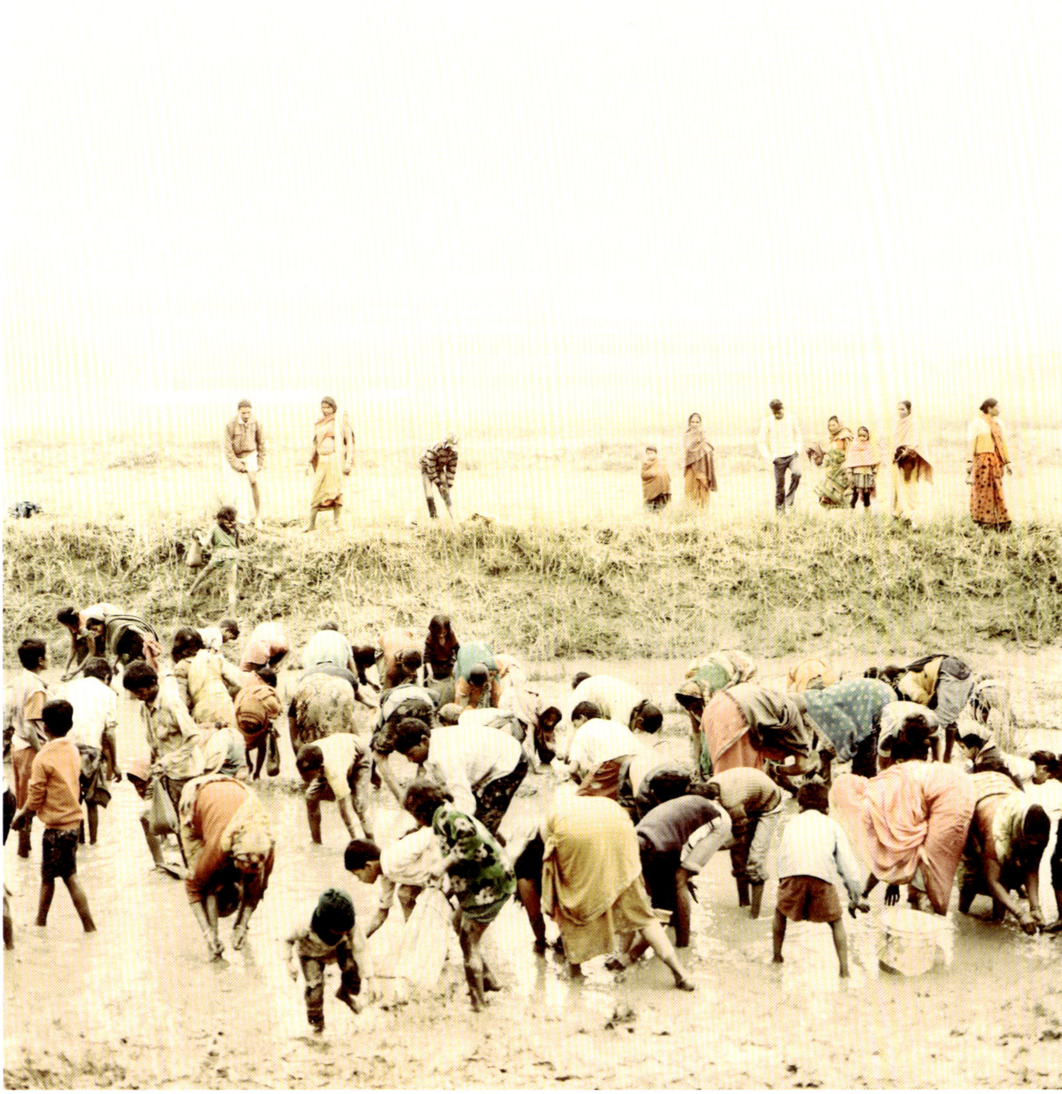

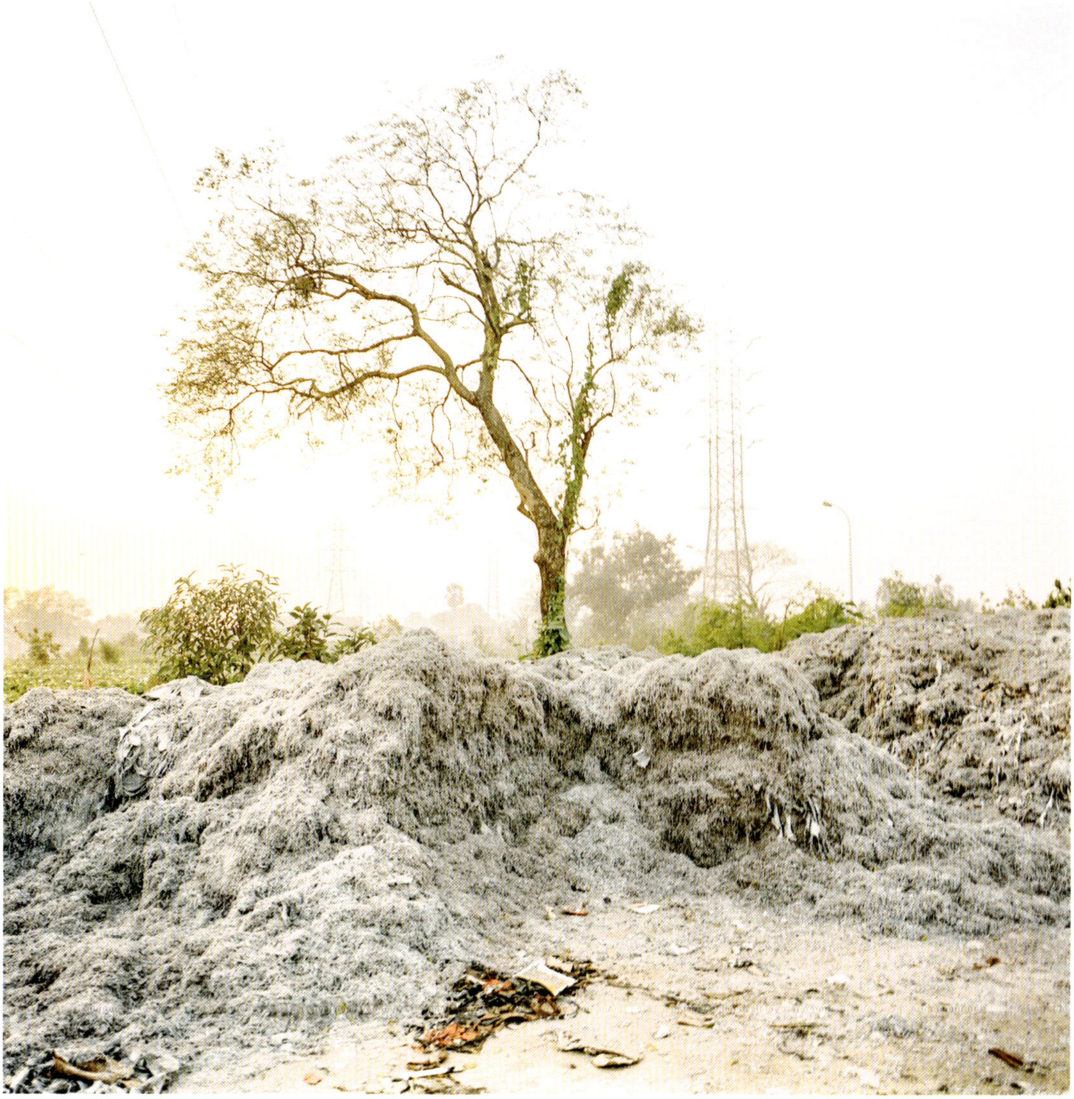

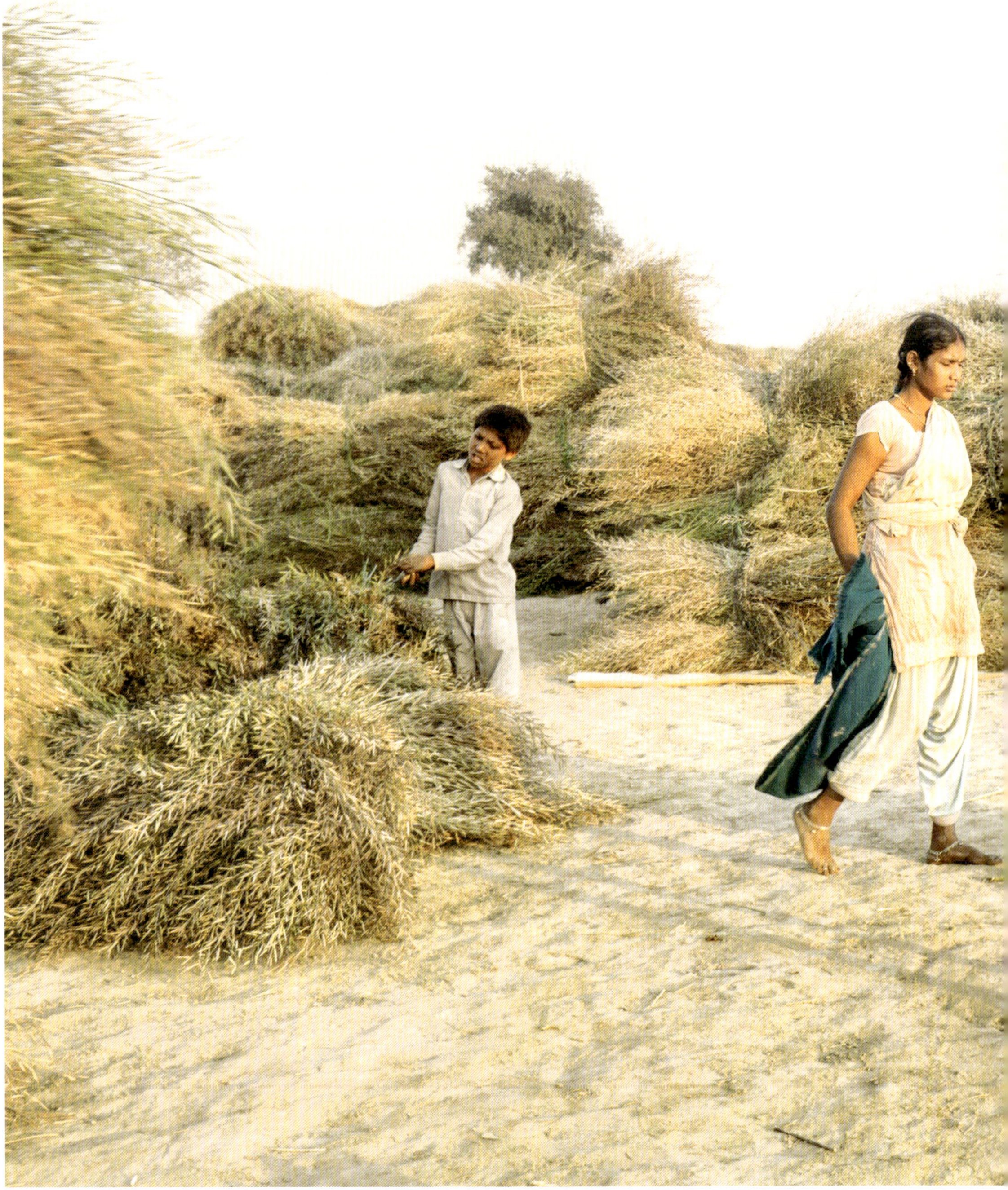

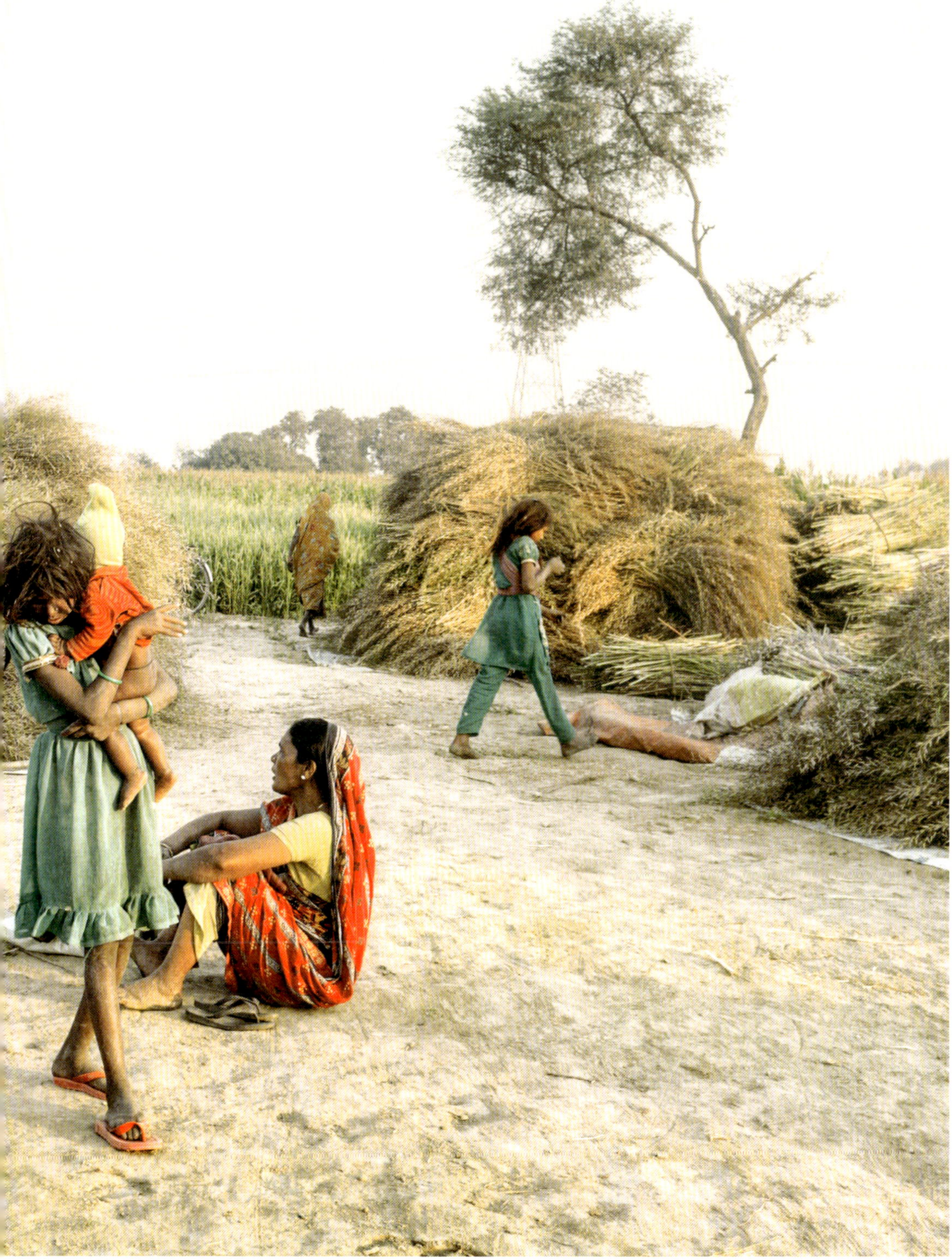

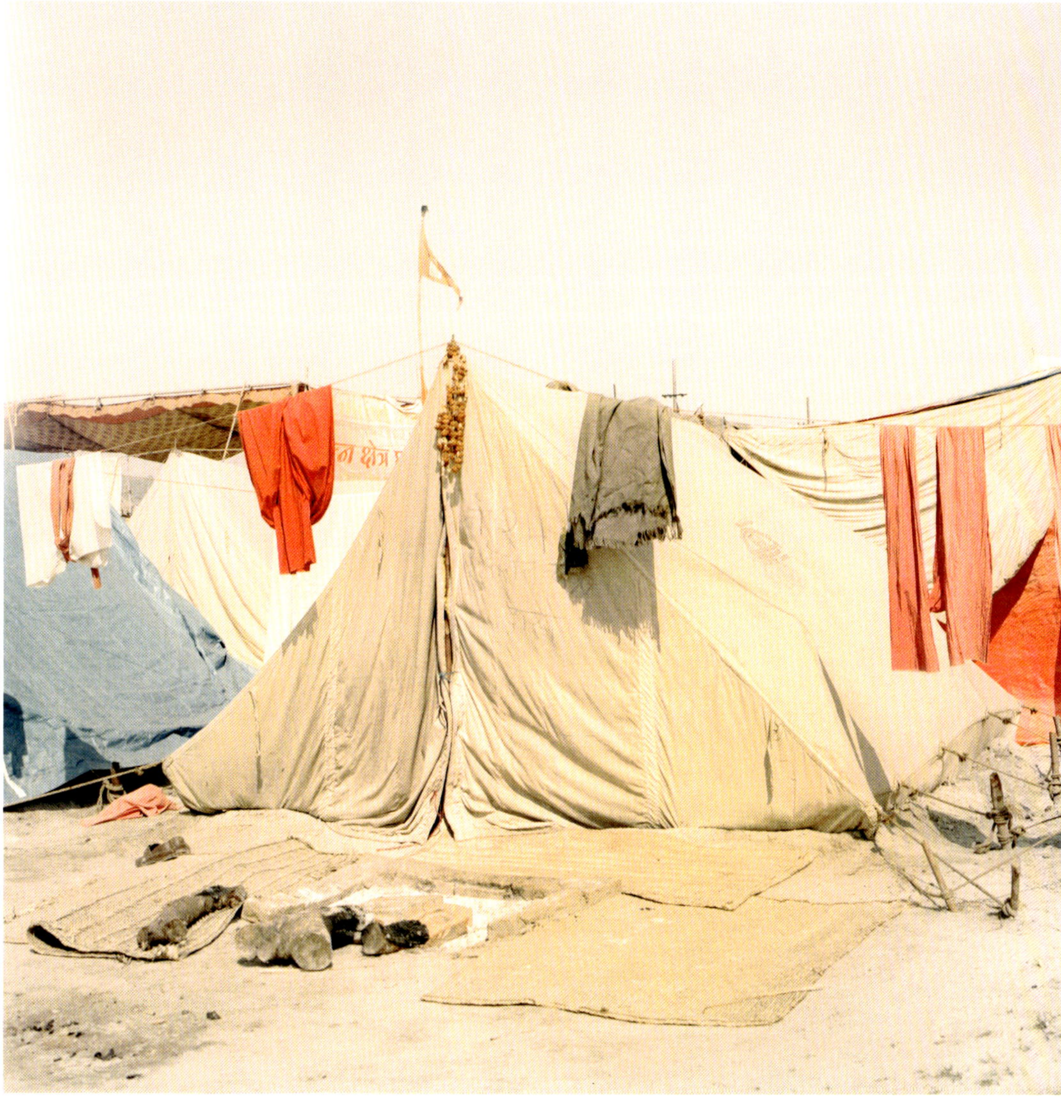

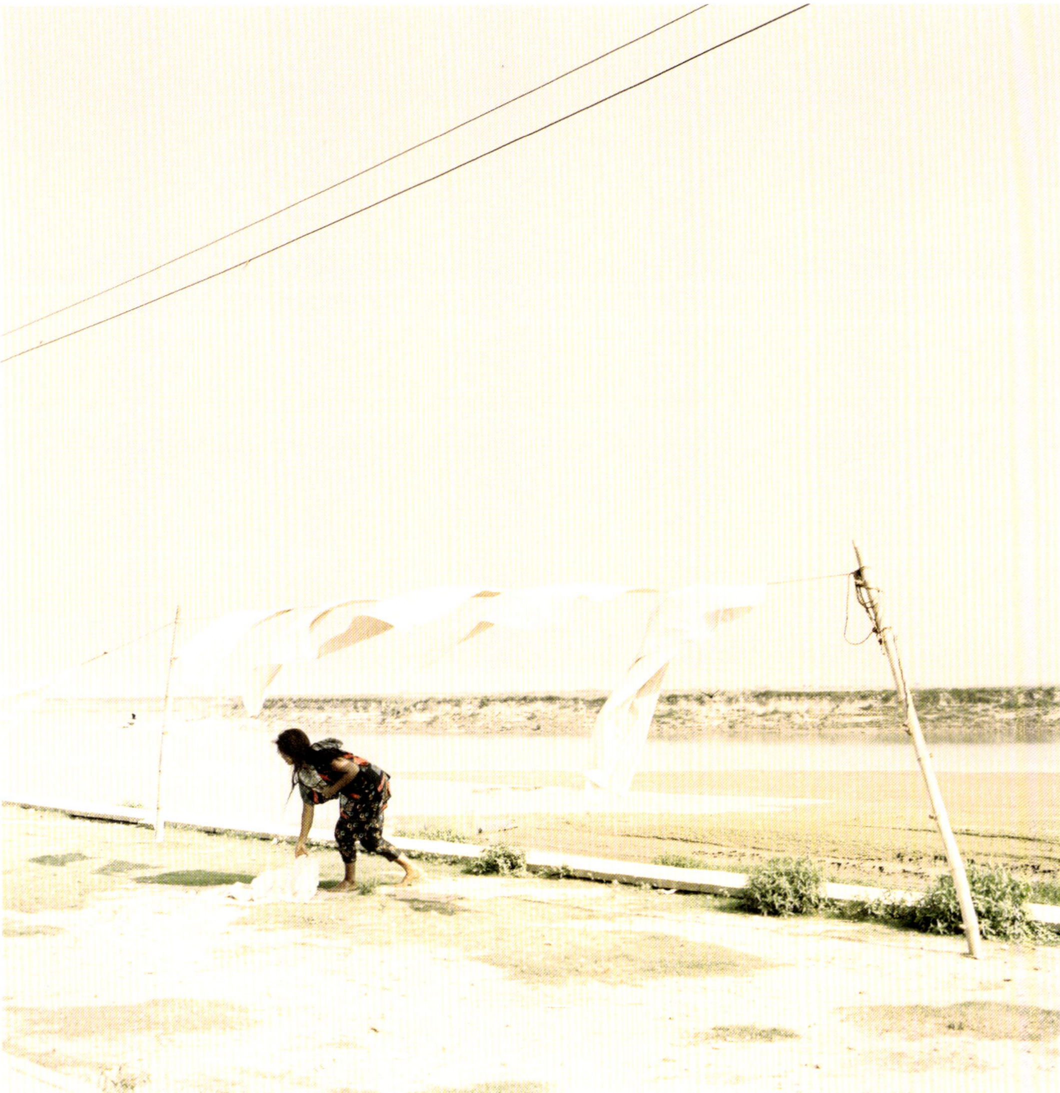

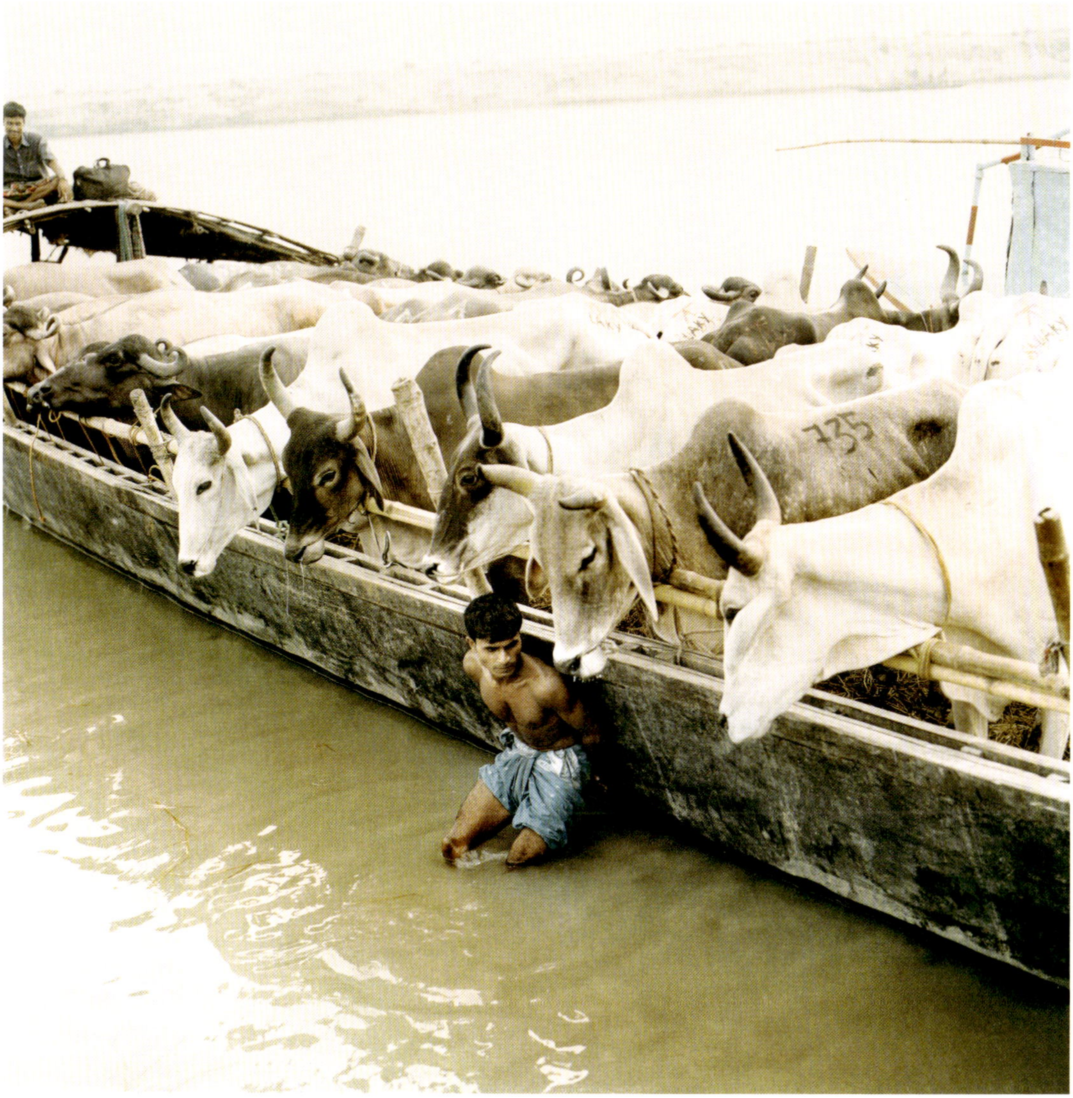
735

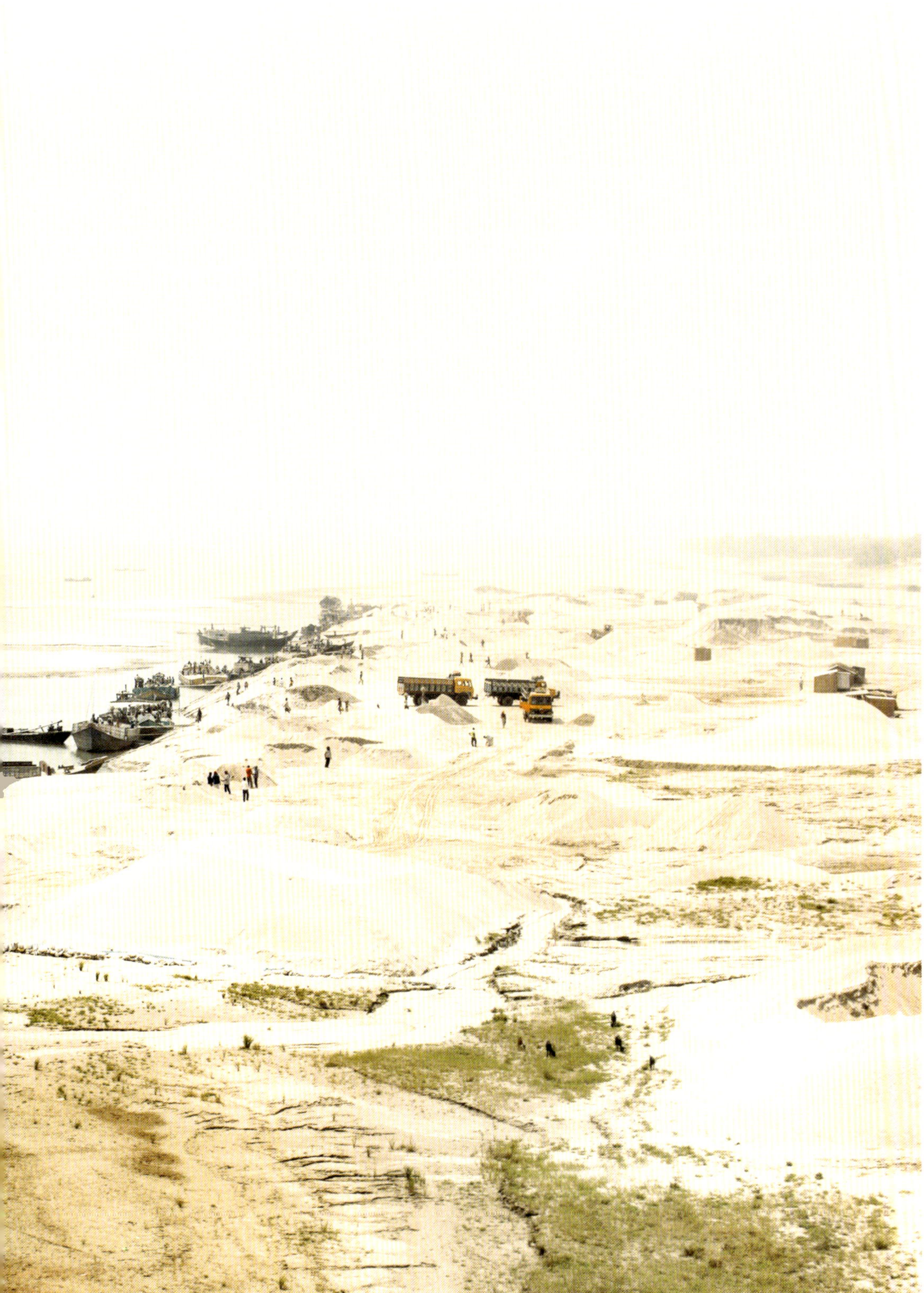

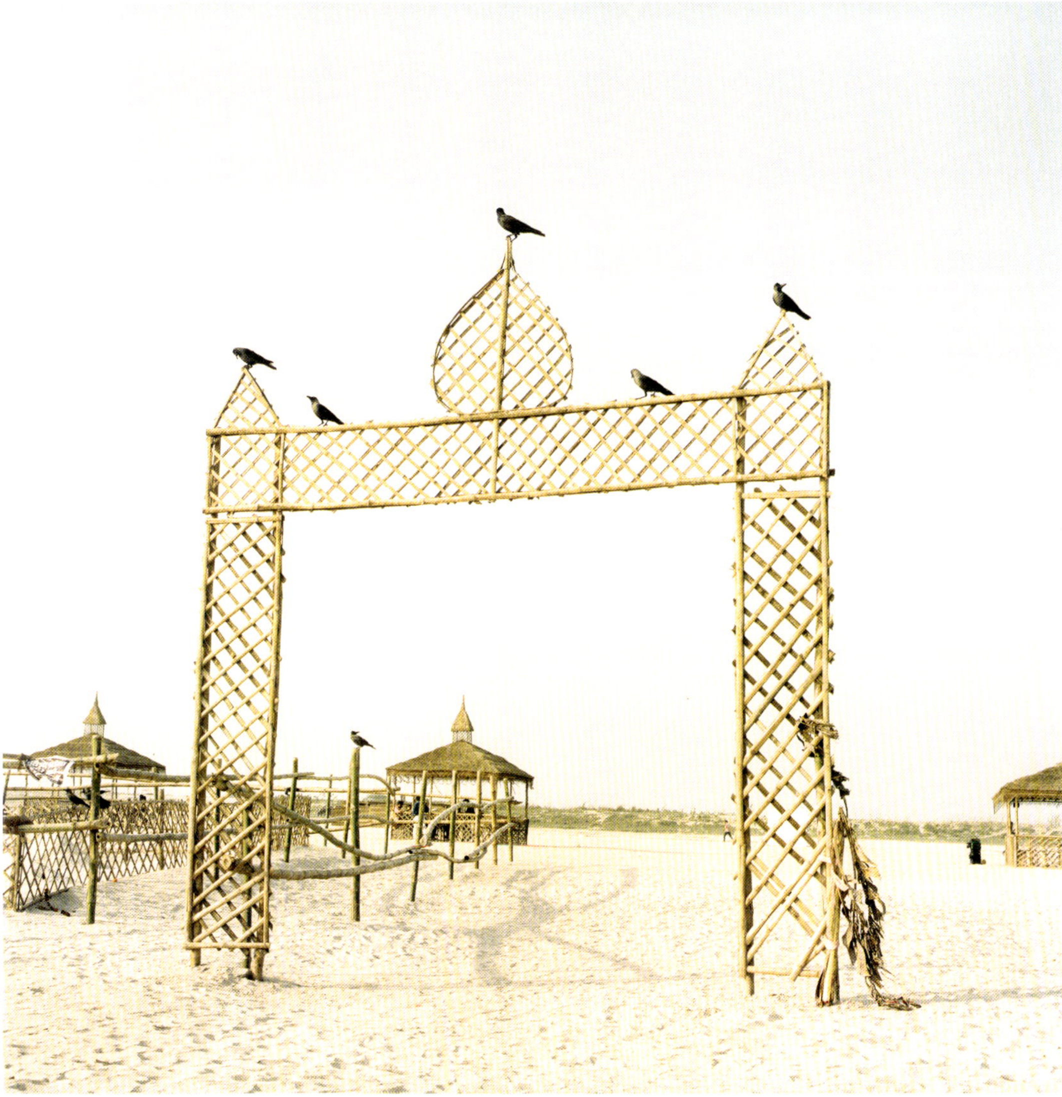

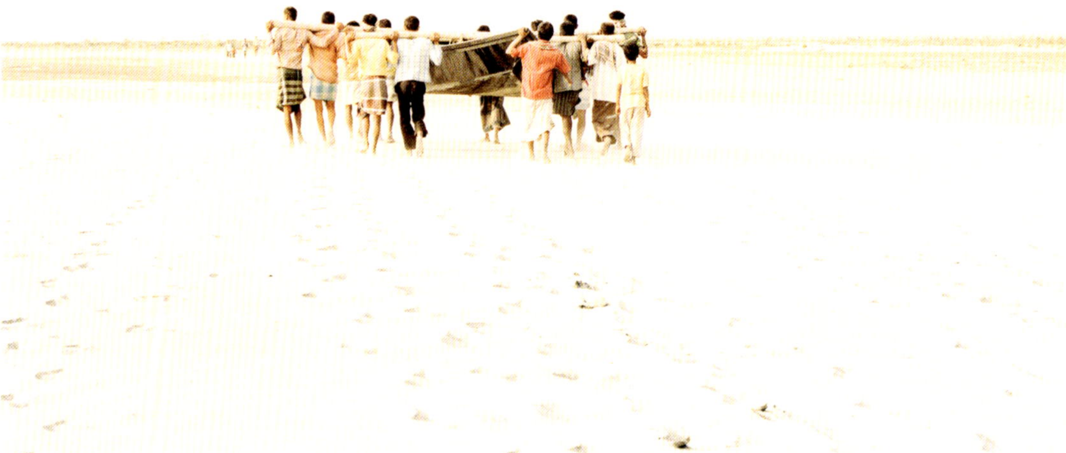

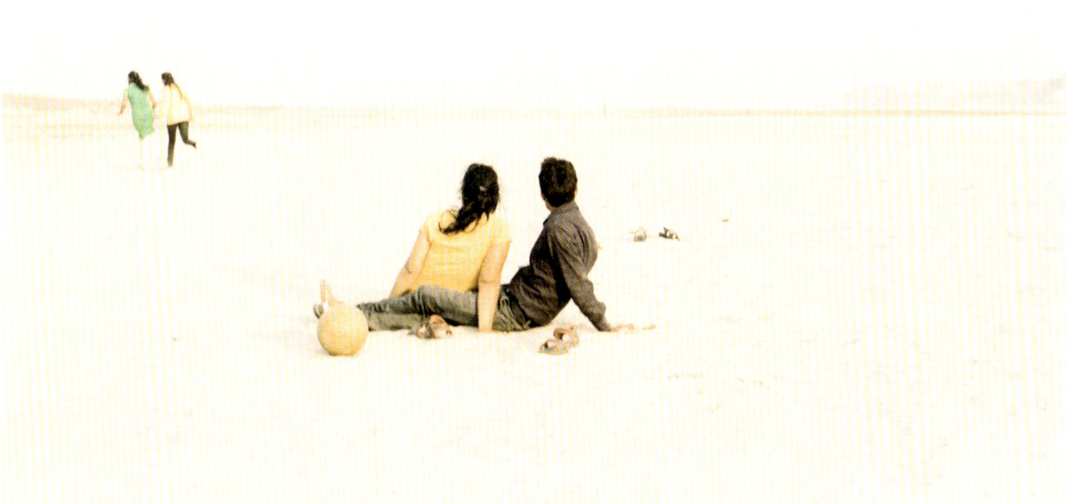

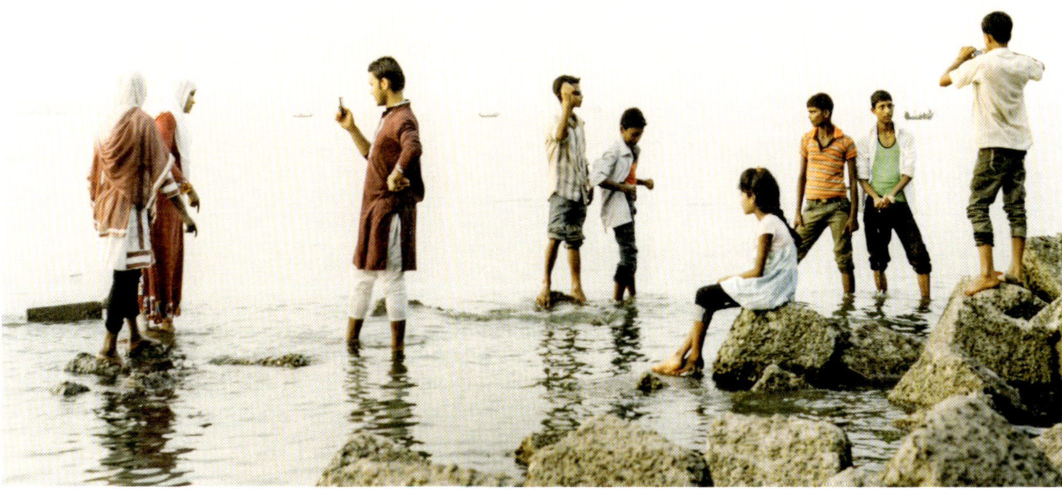

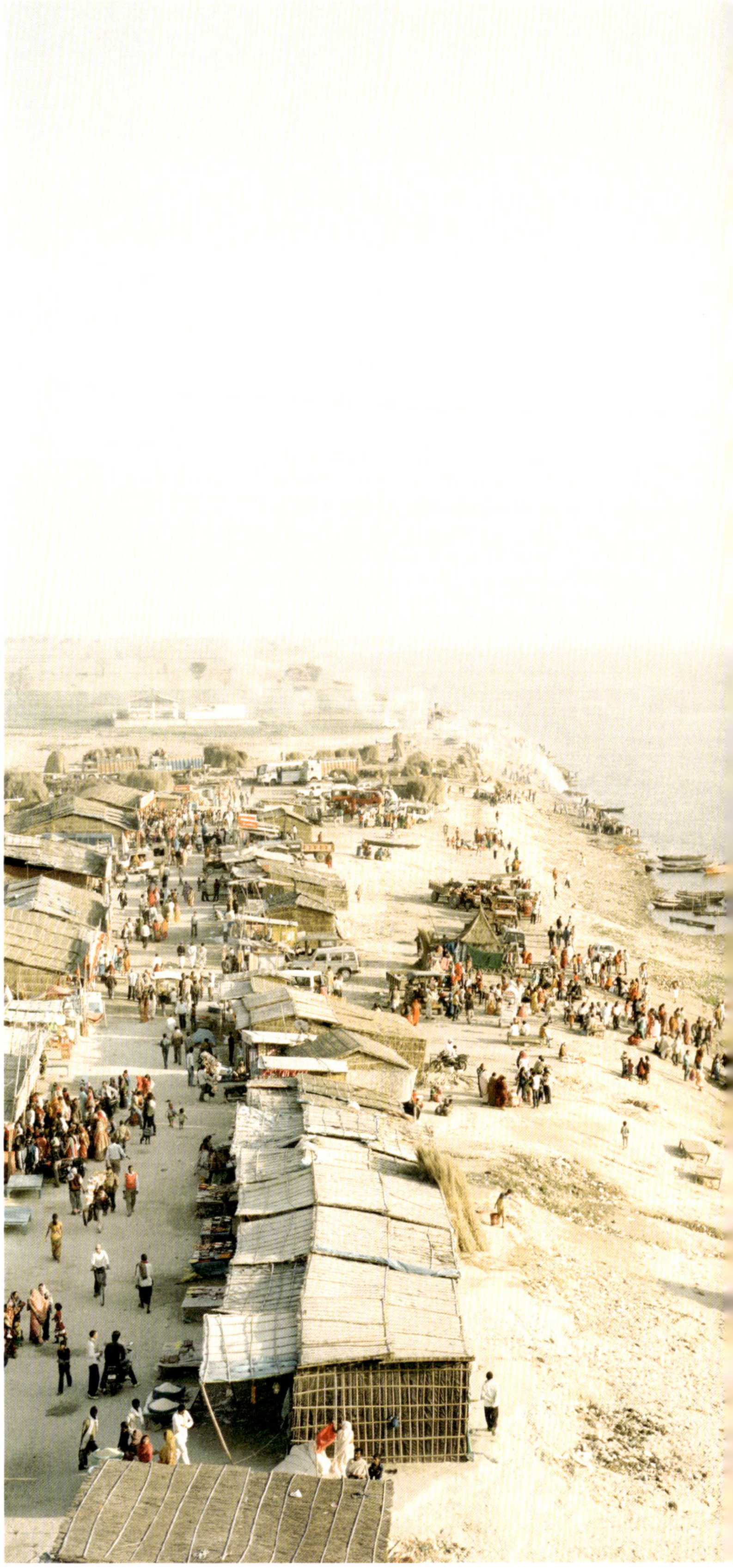

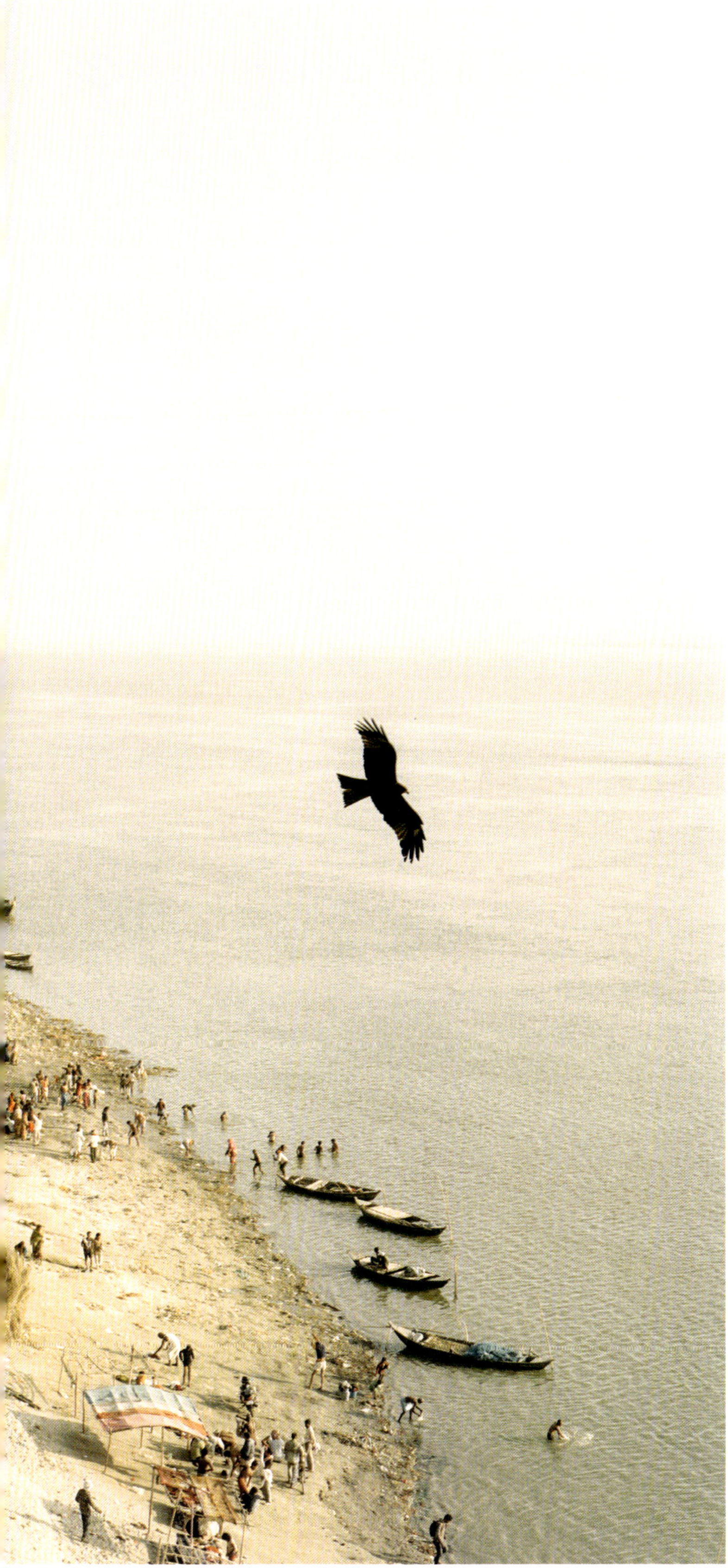

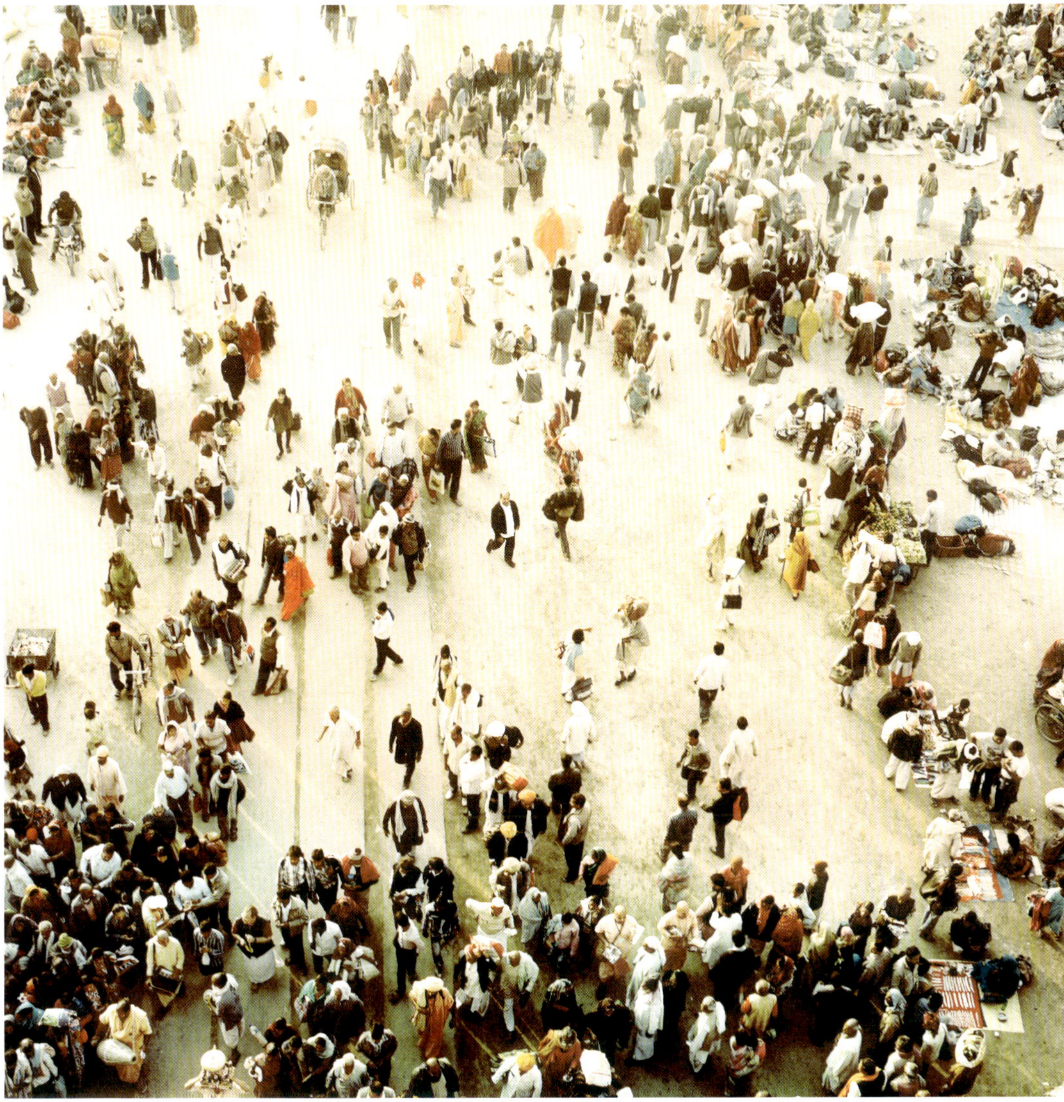

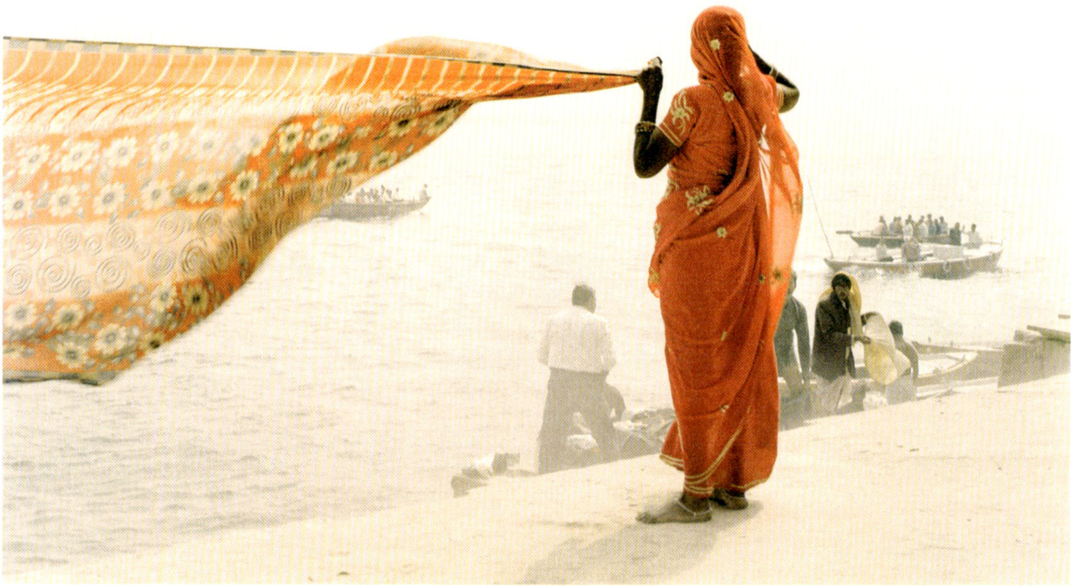

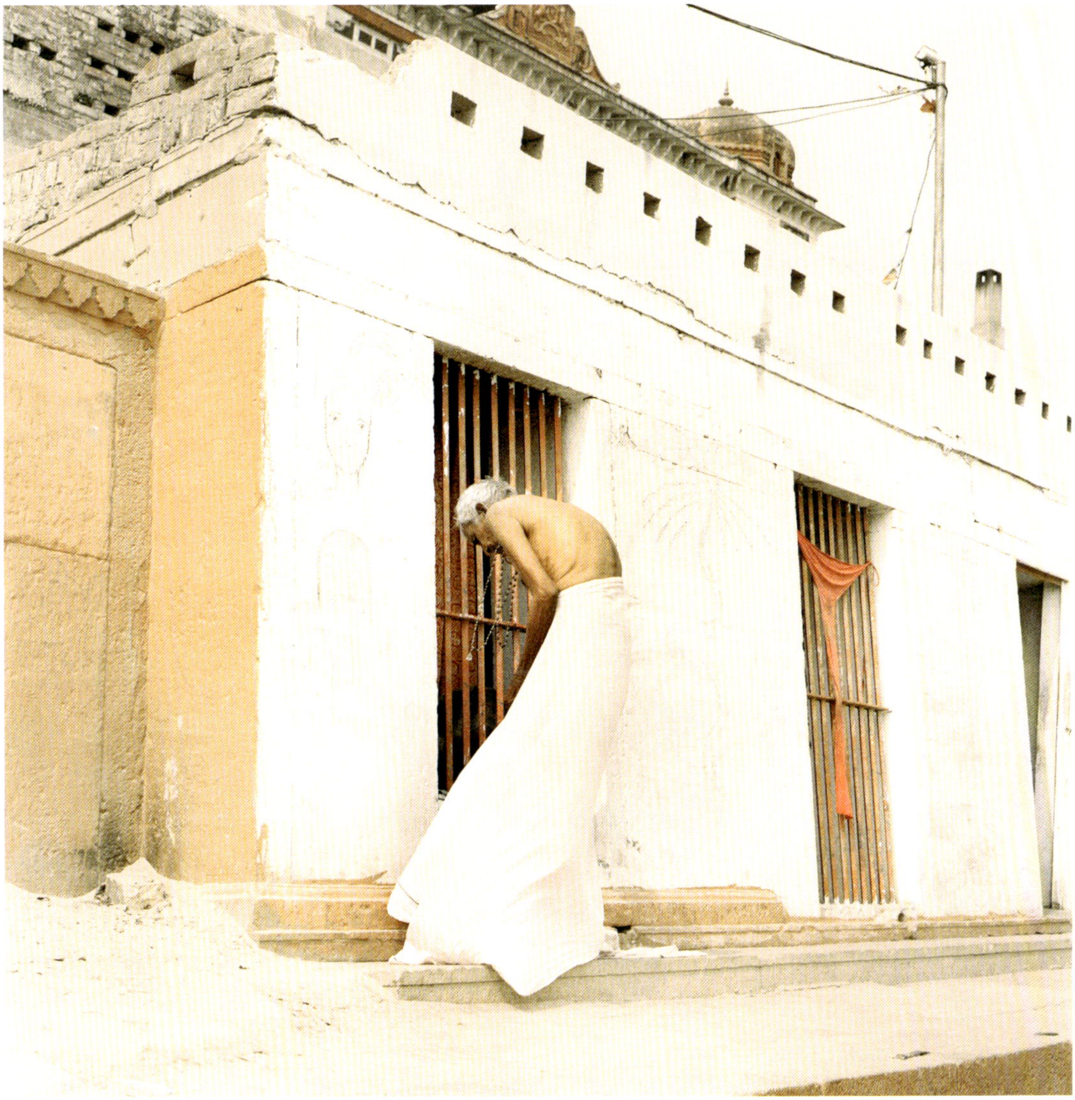

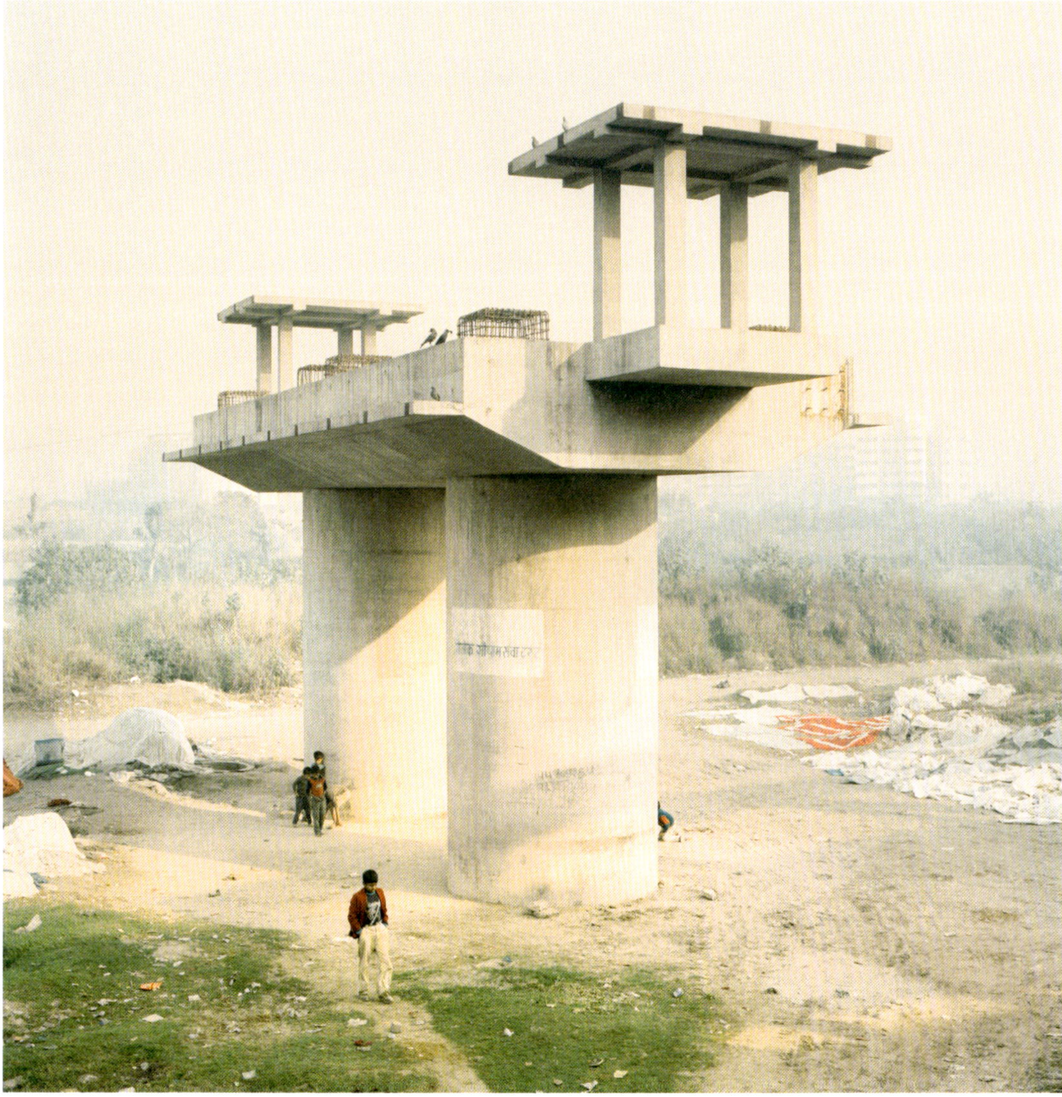

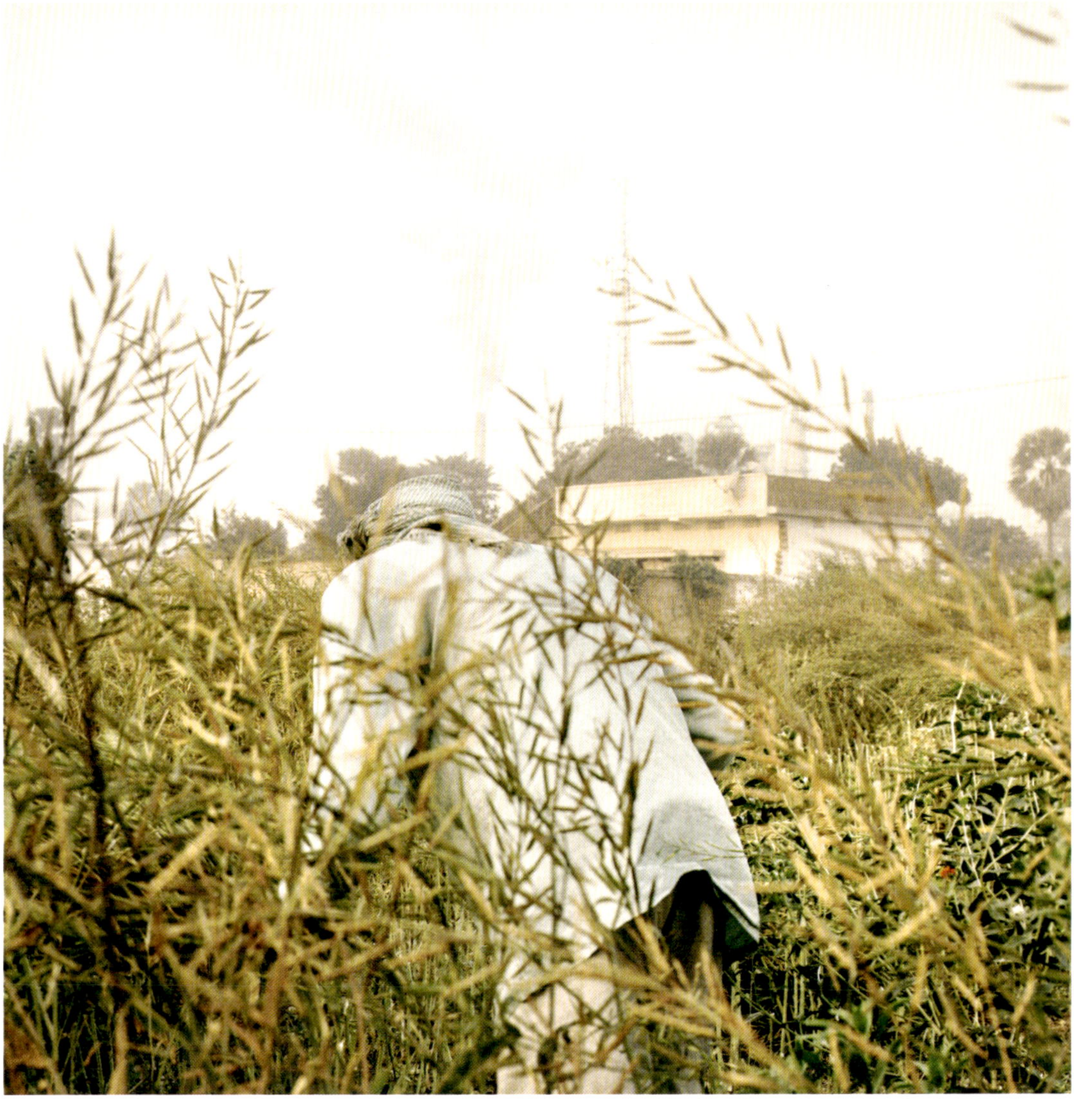

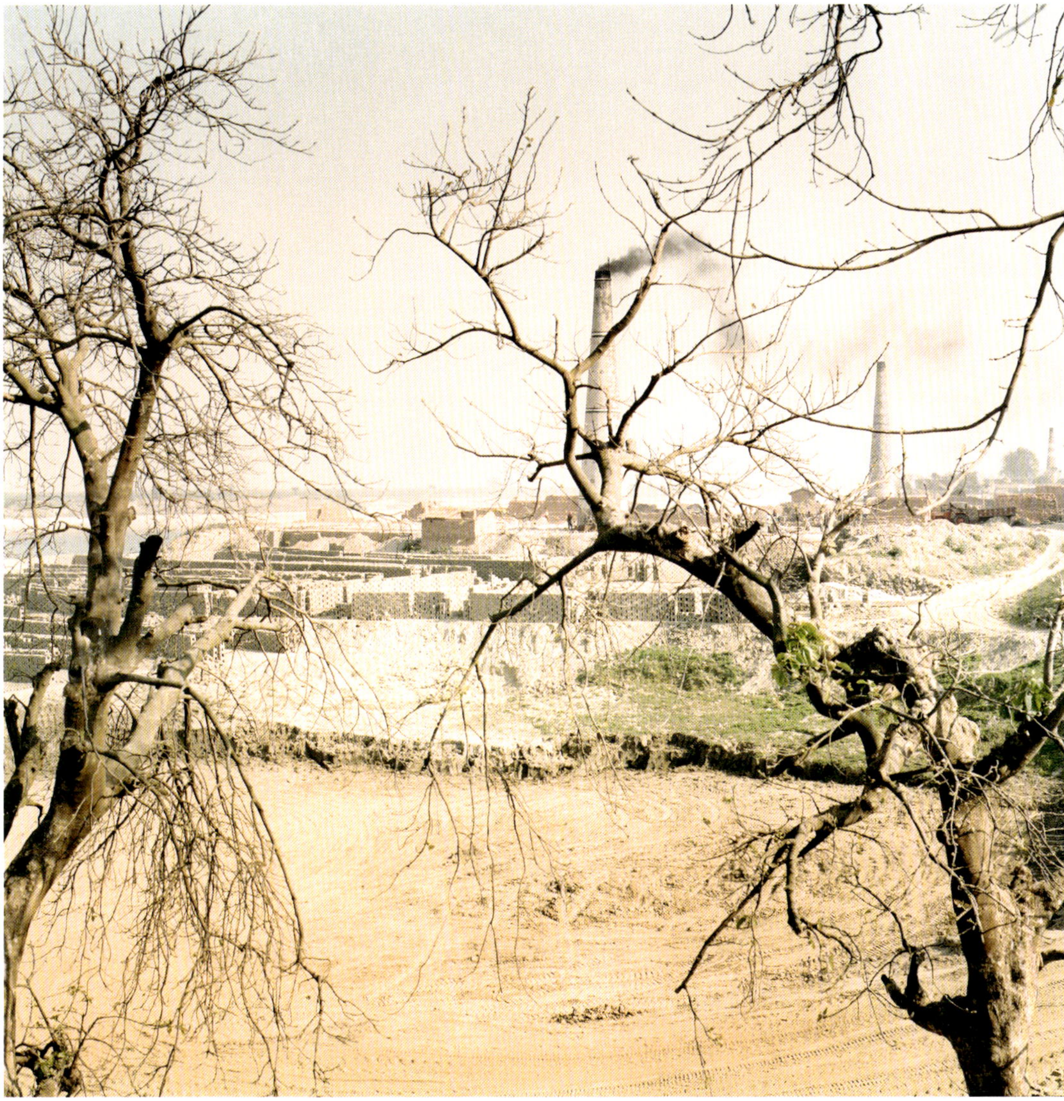

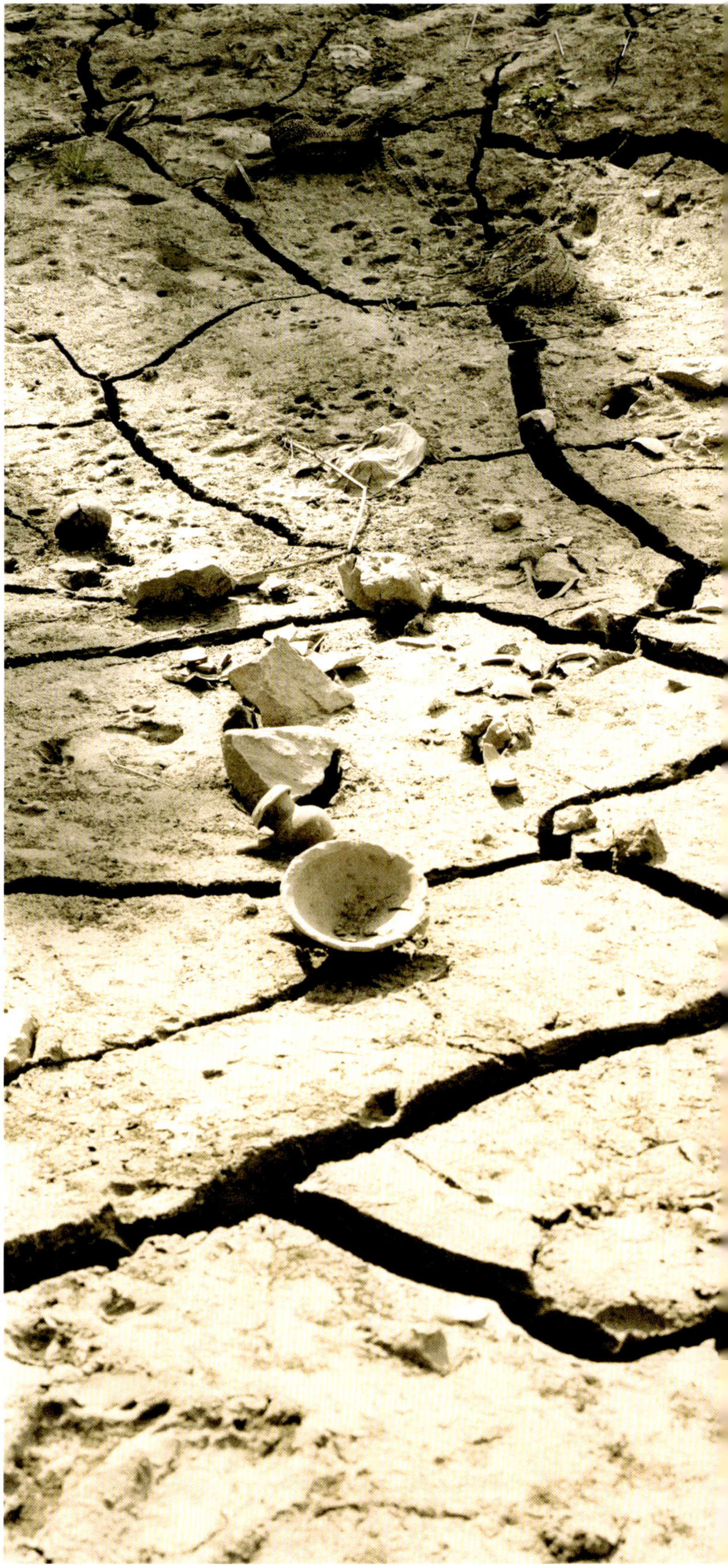

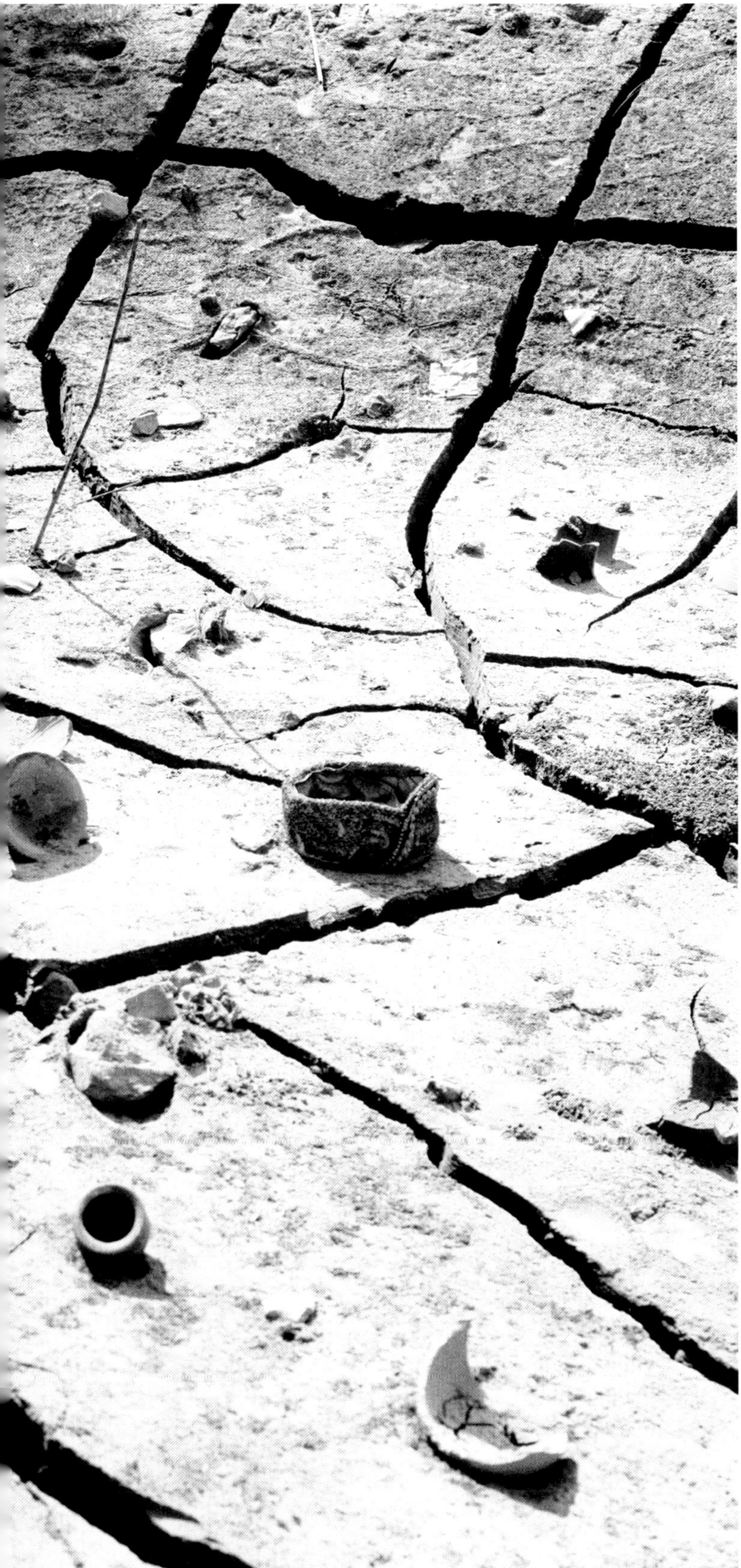

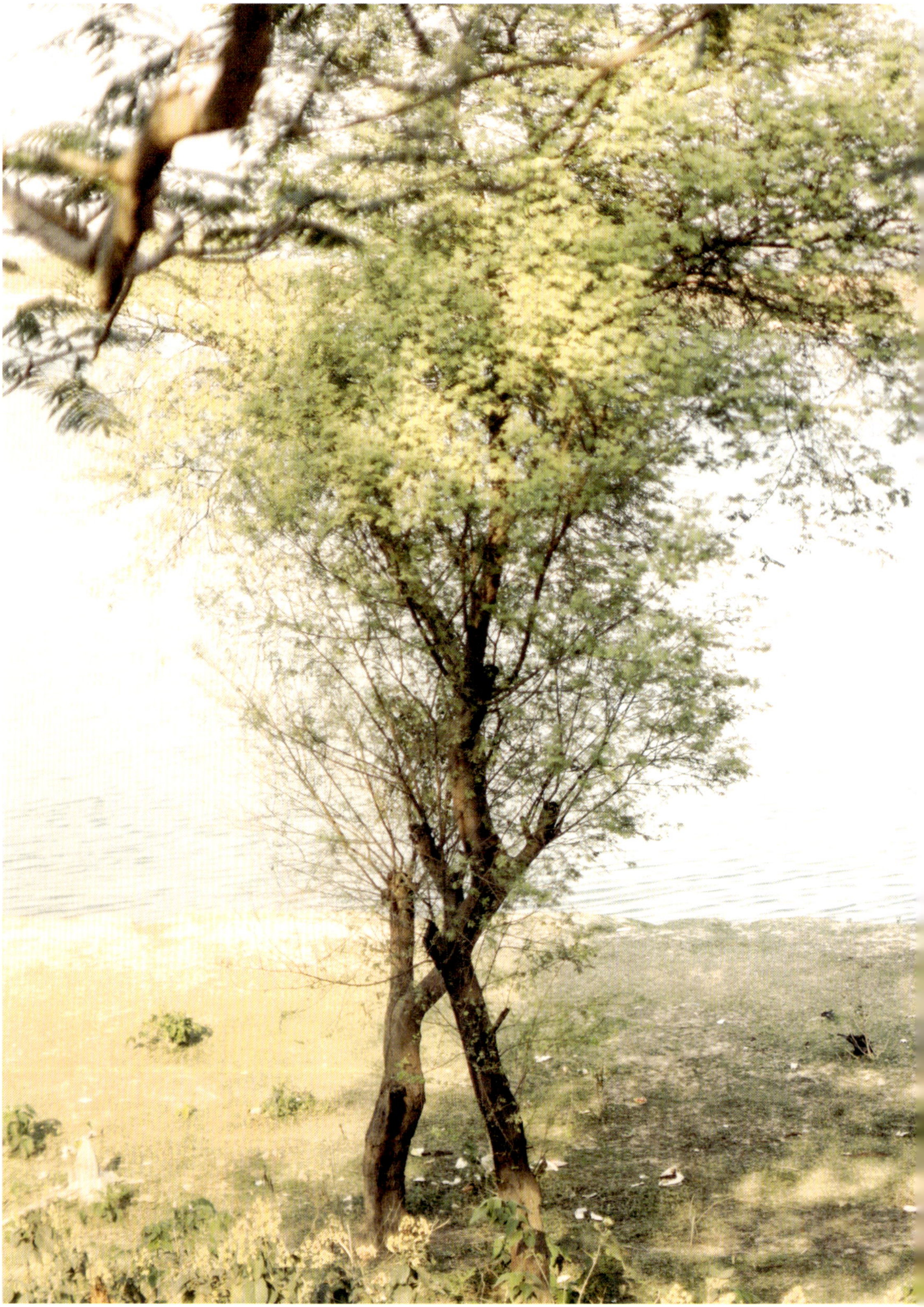

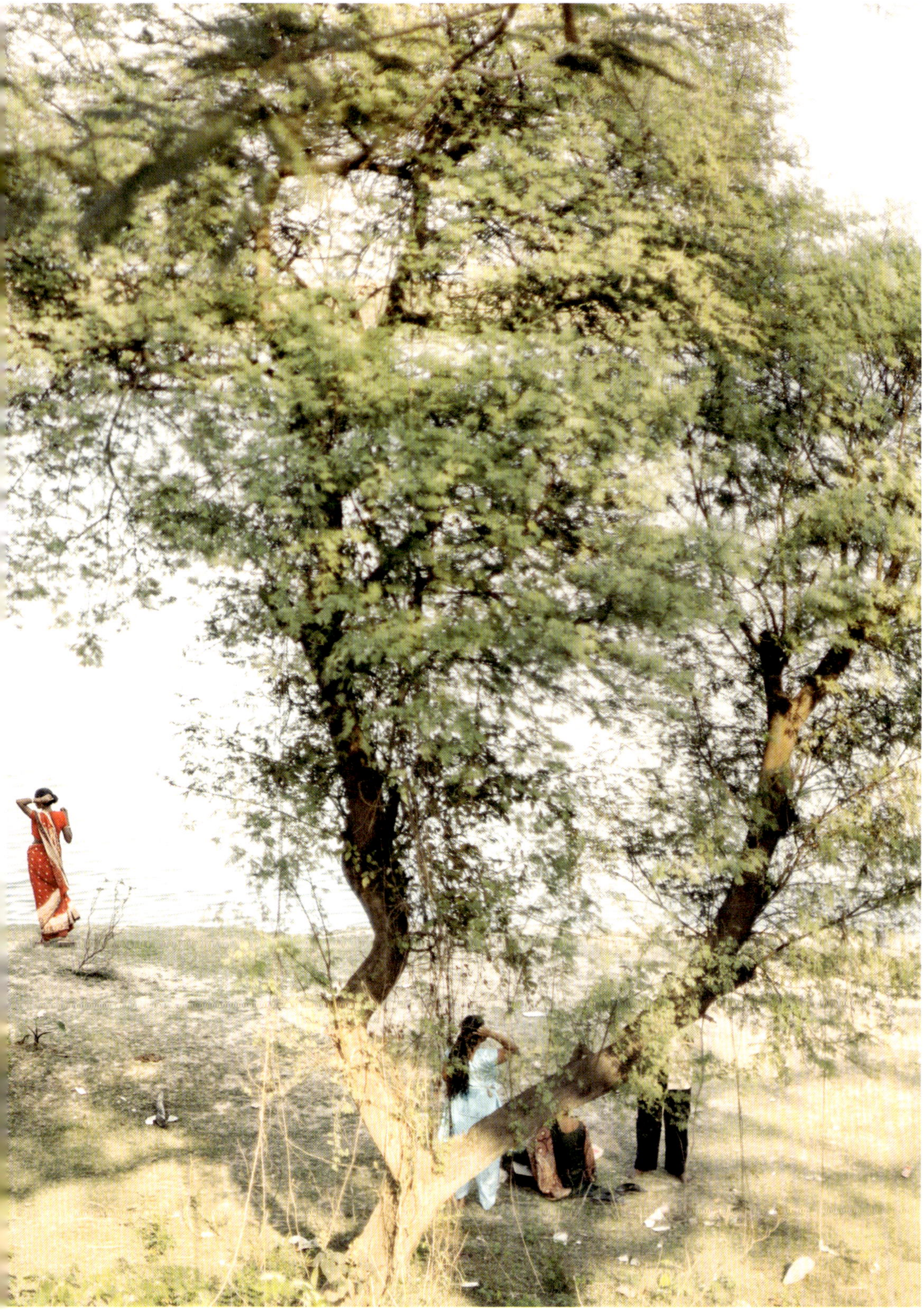

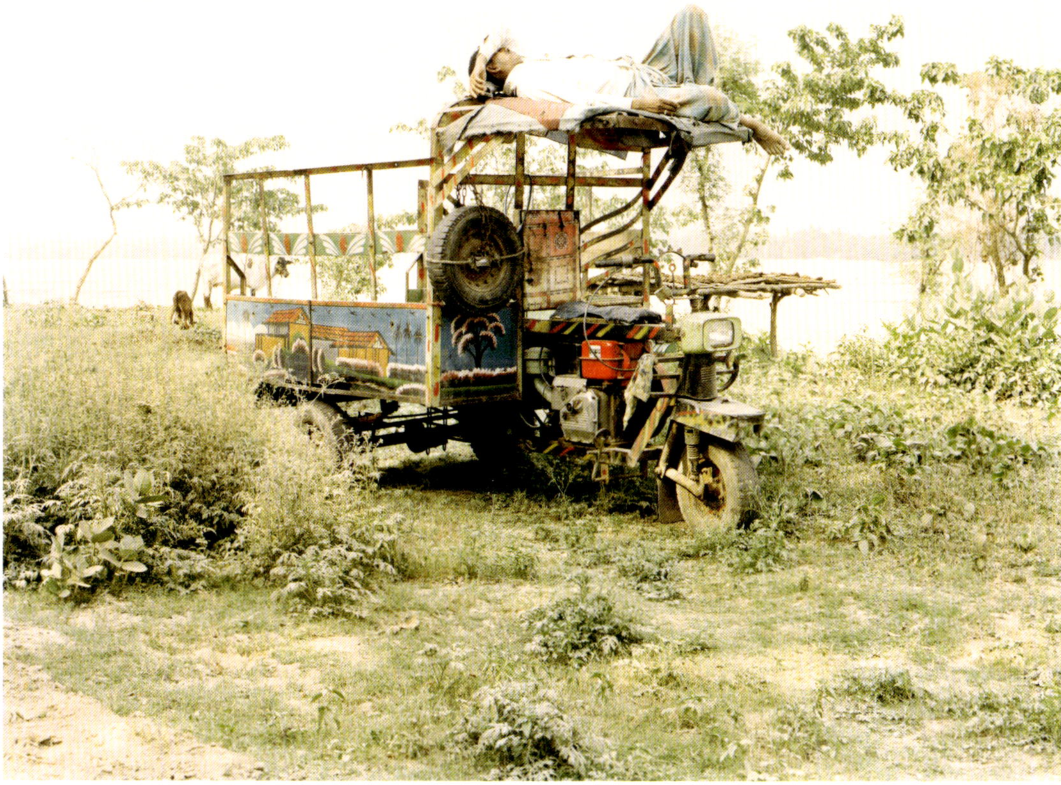

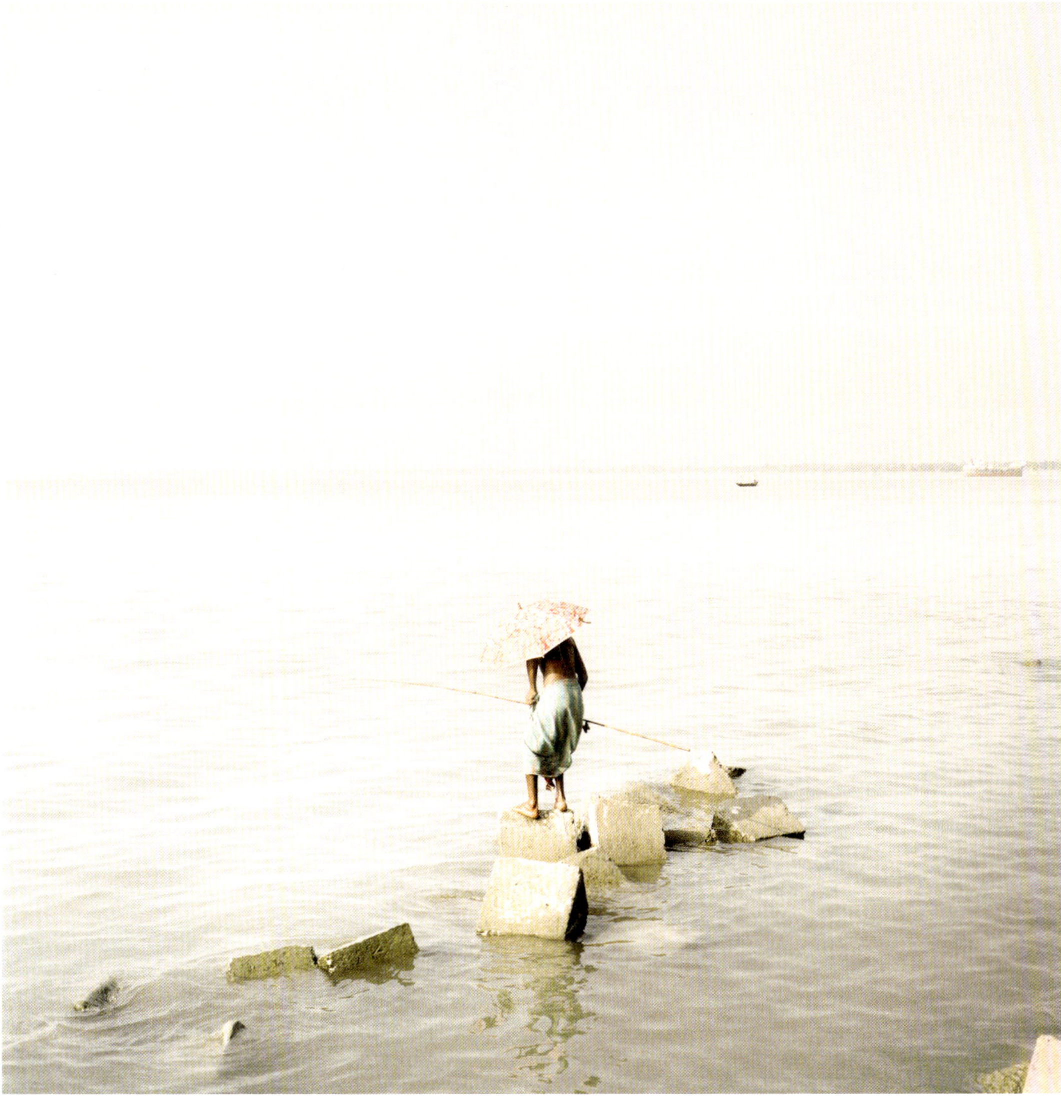

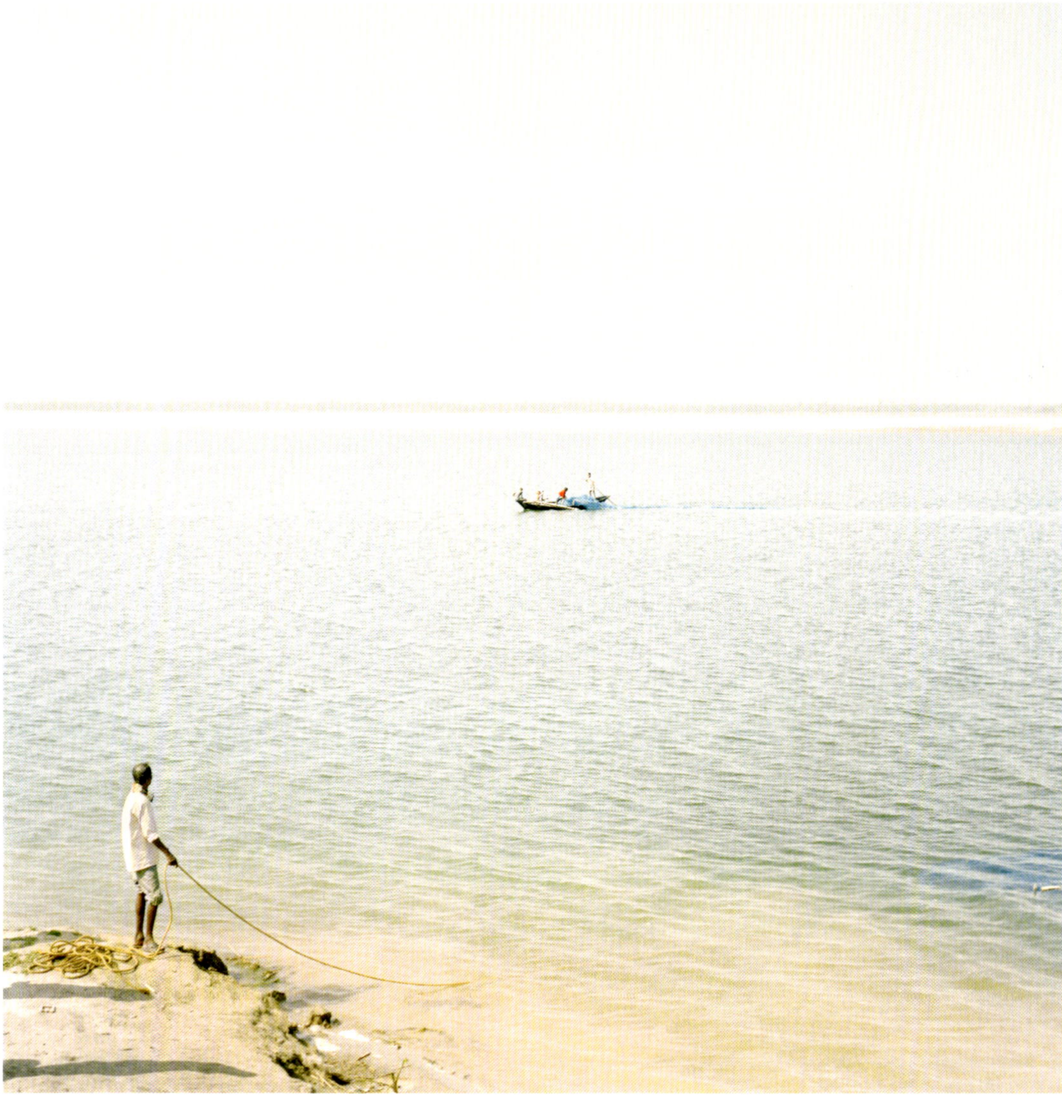

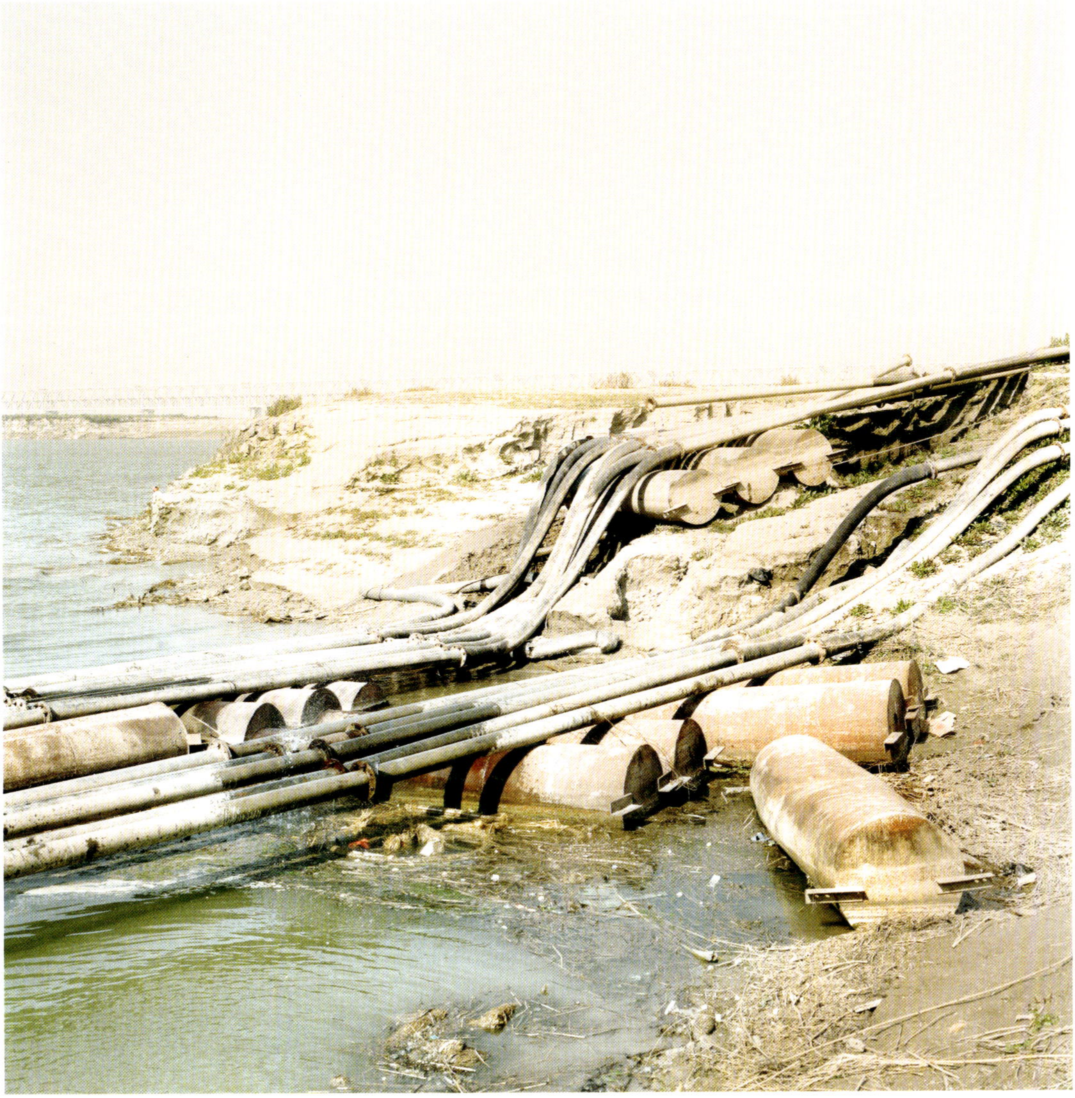

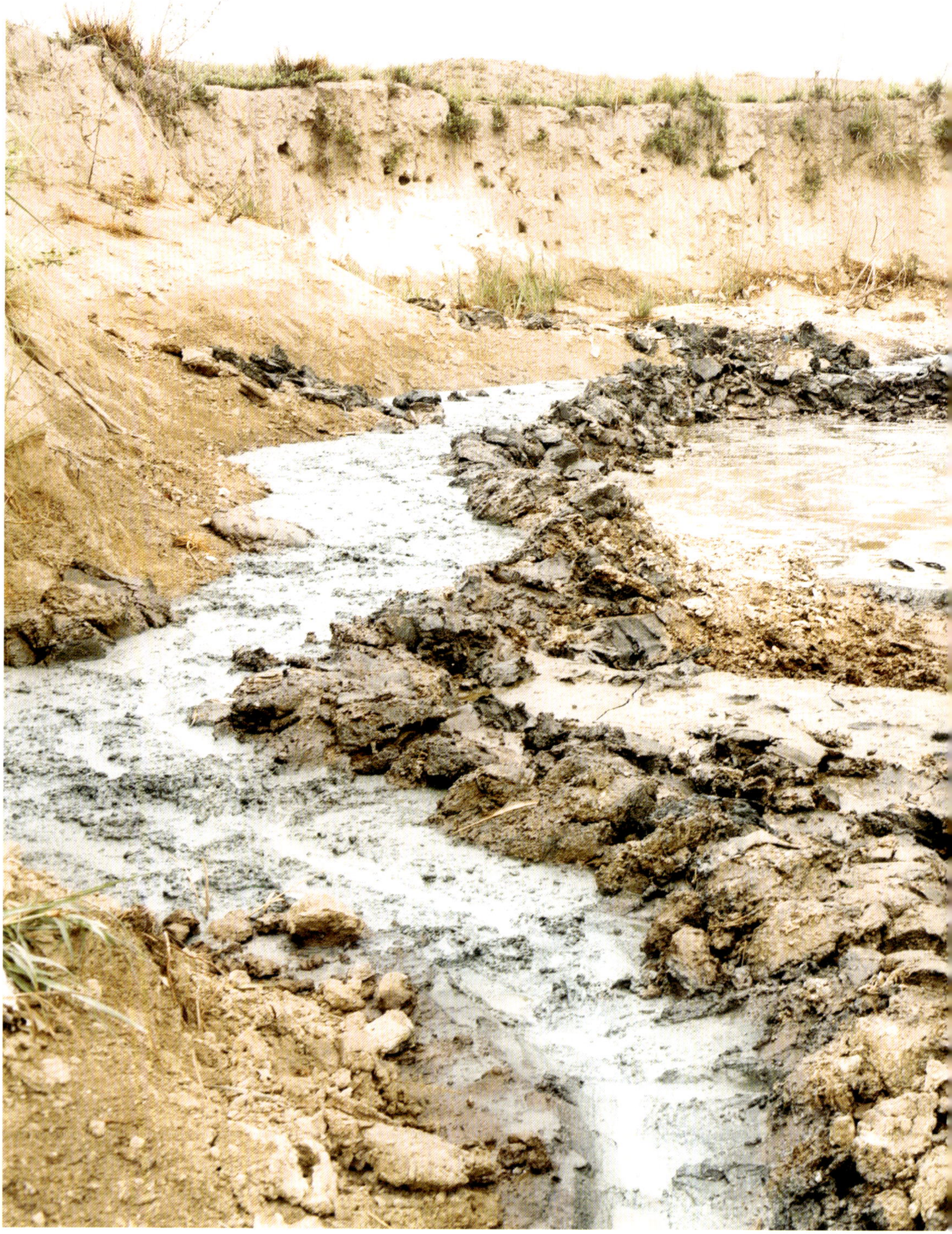

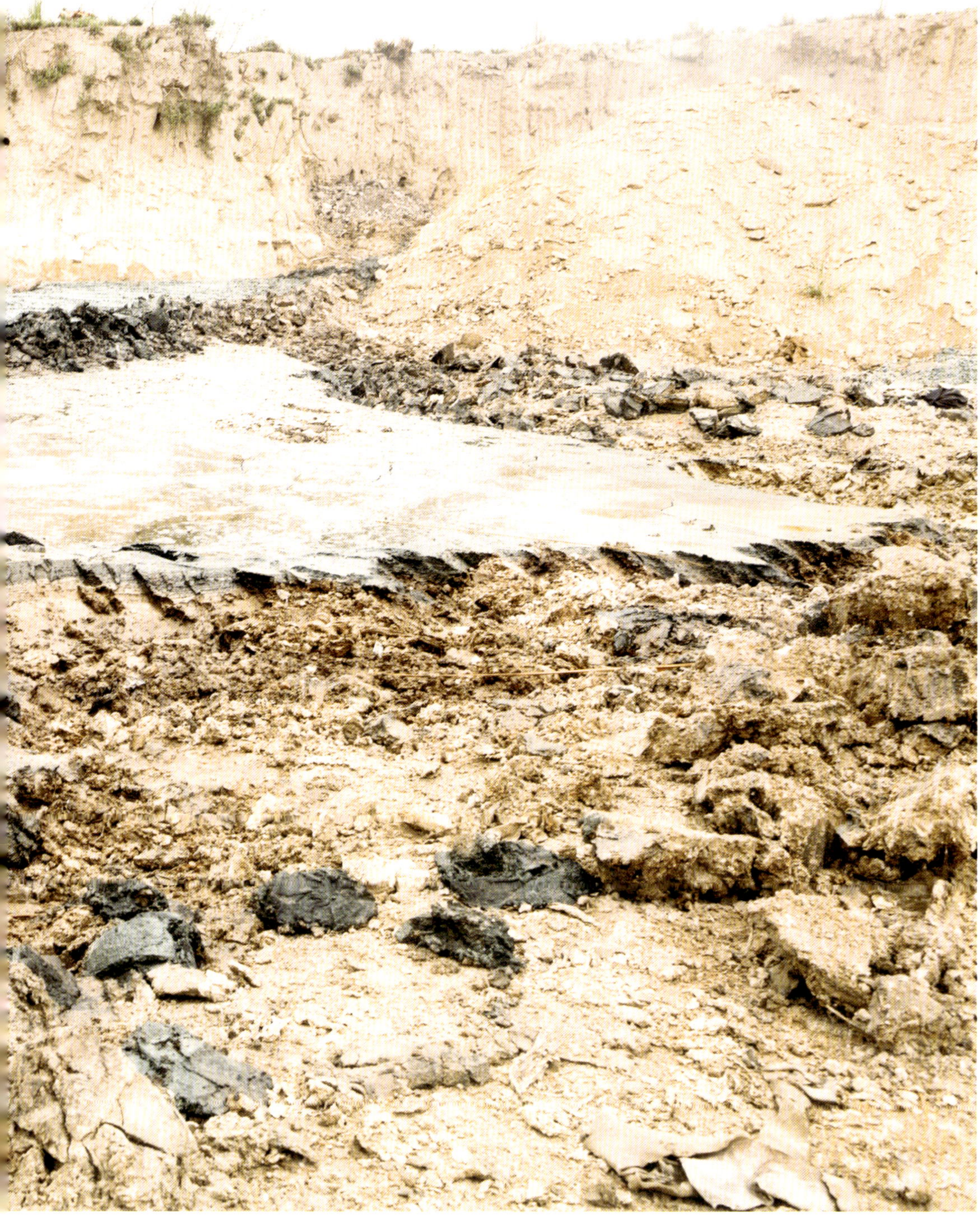

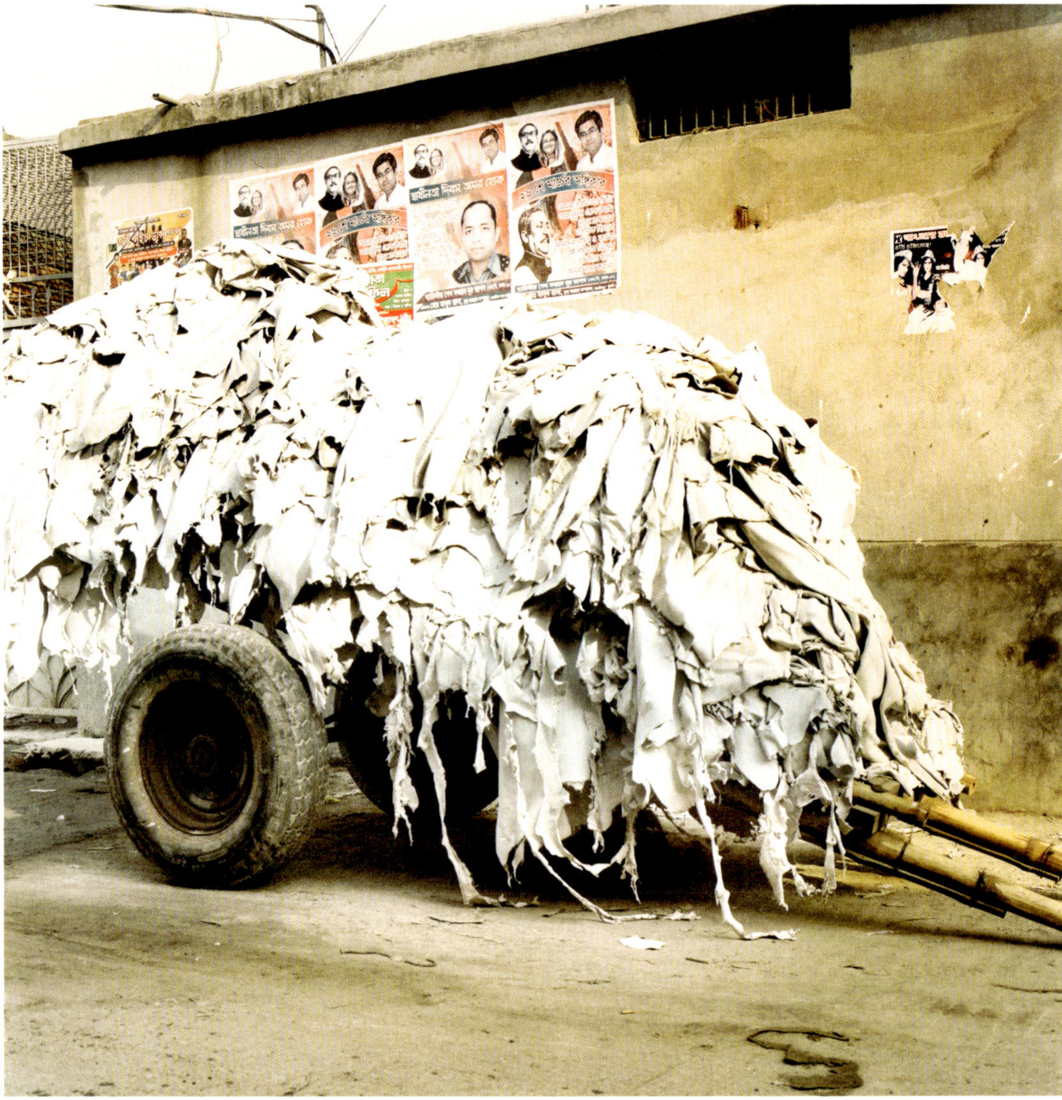

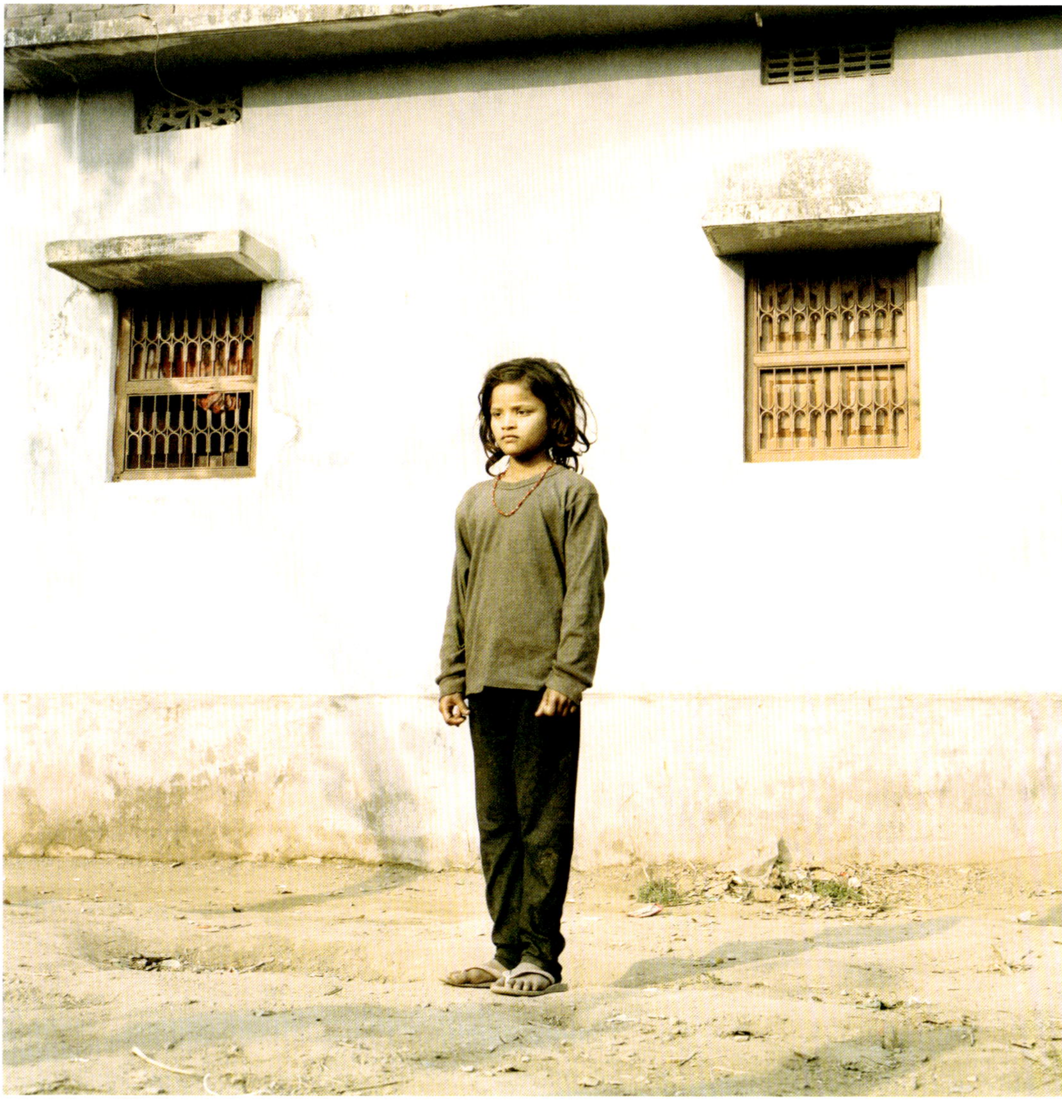

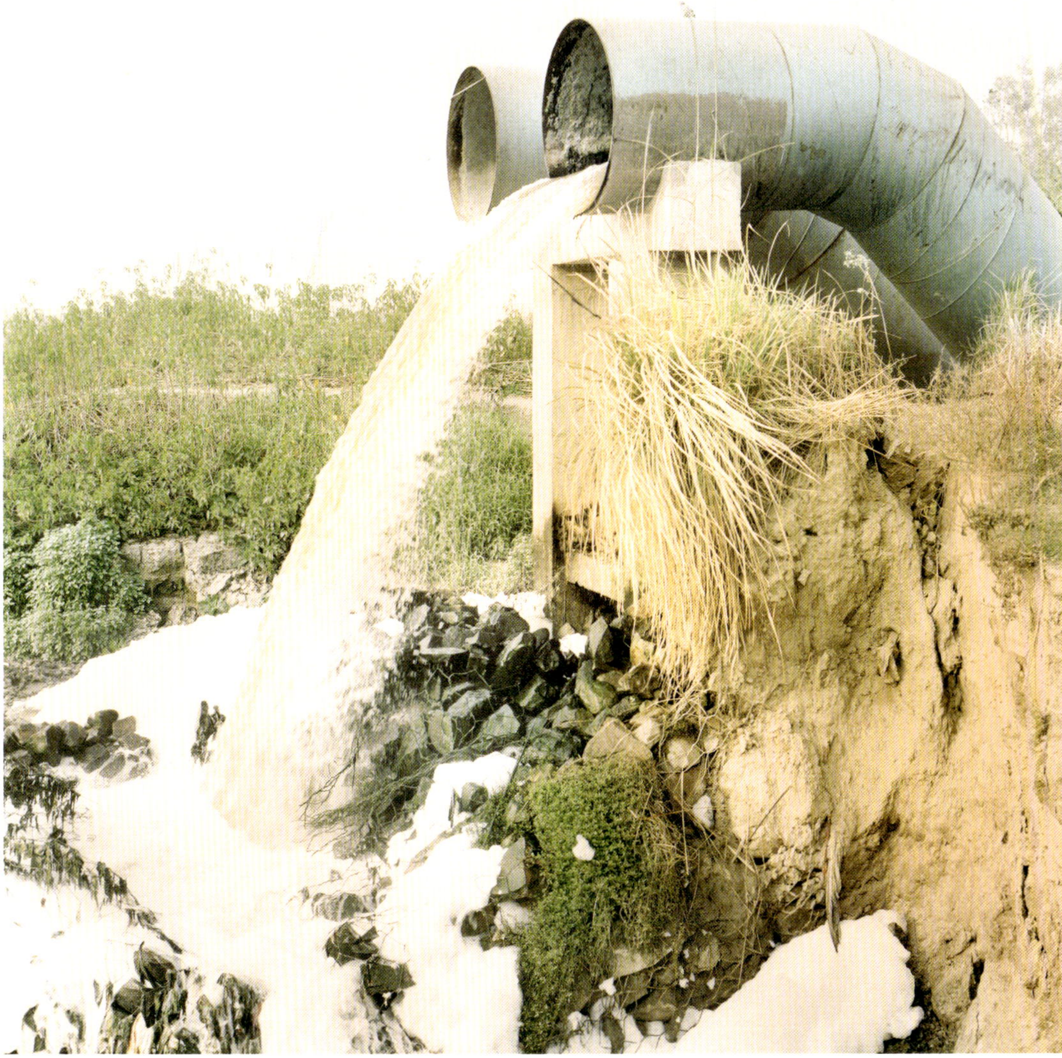

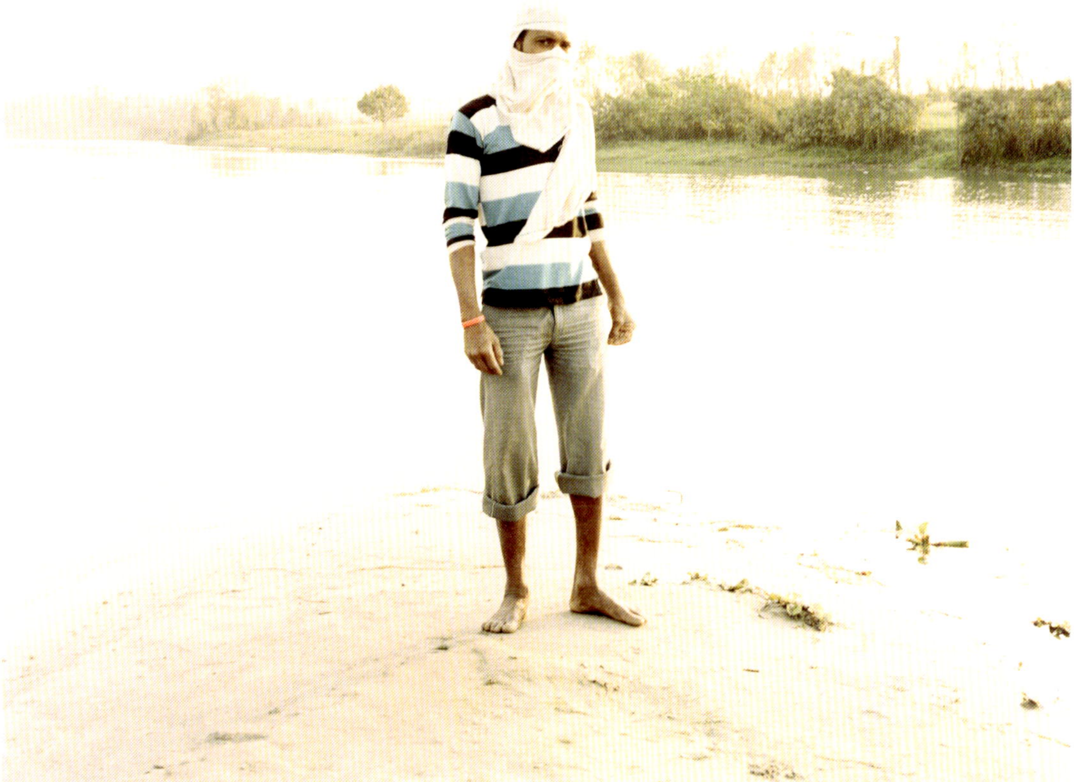

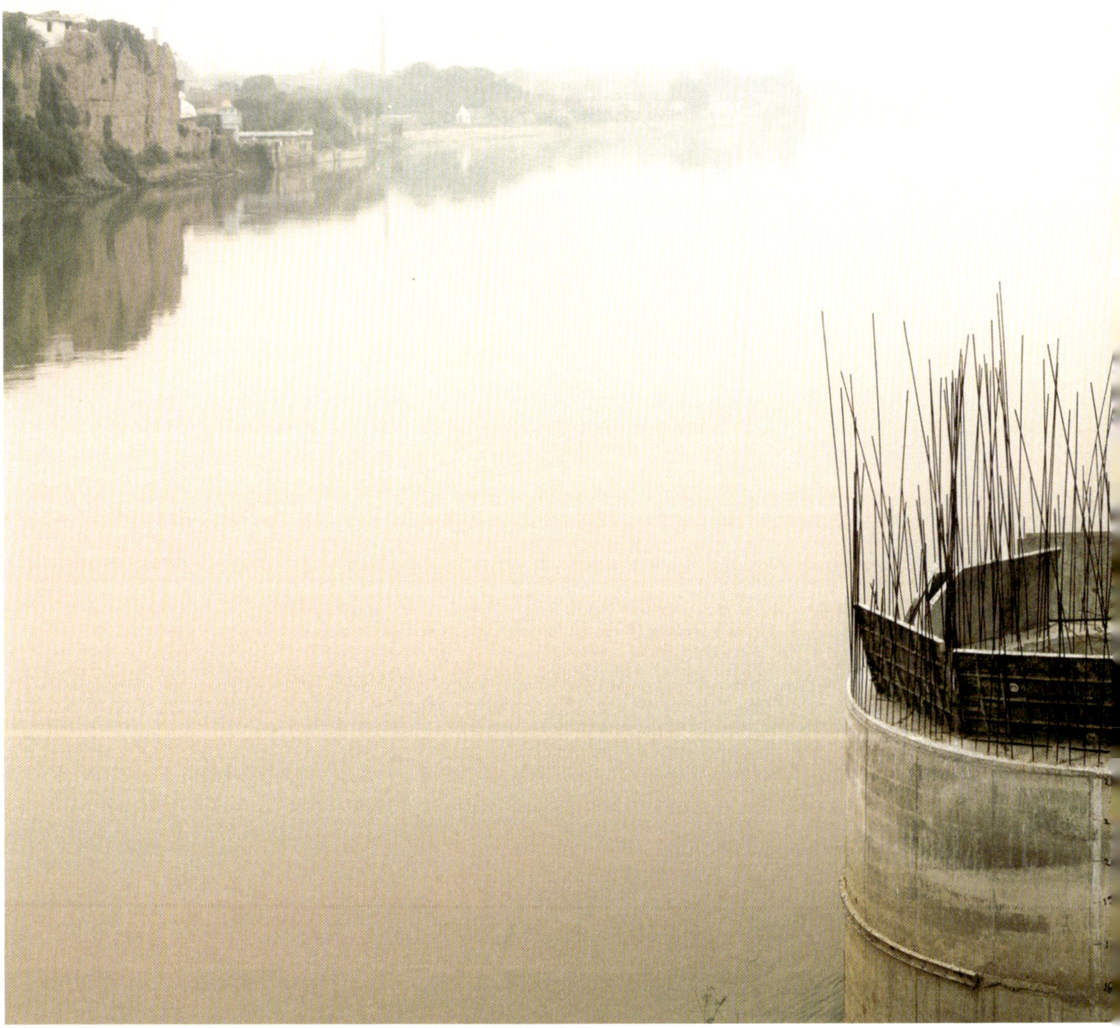

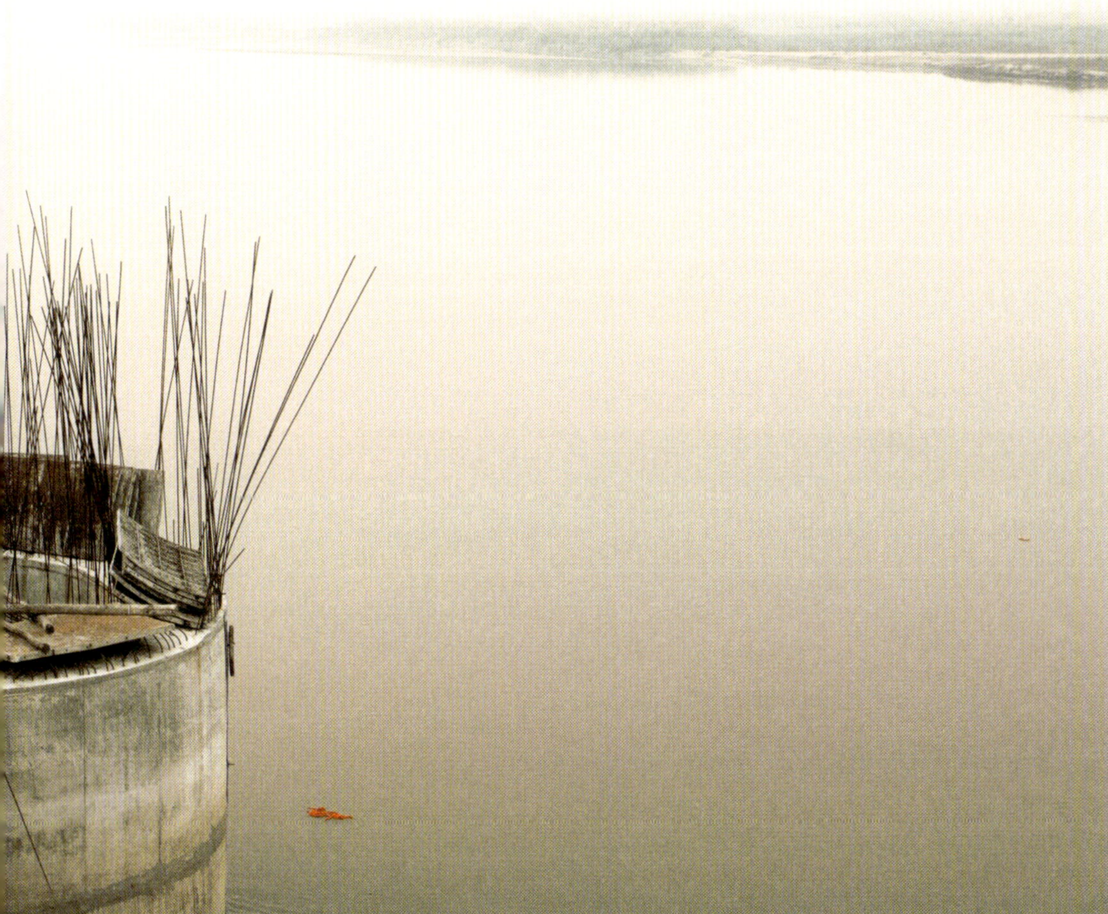

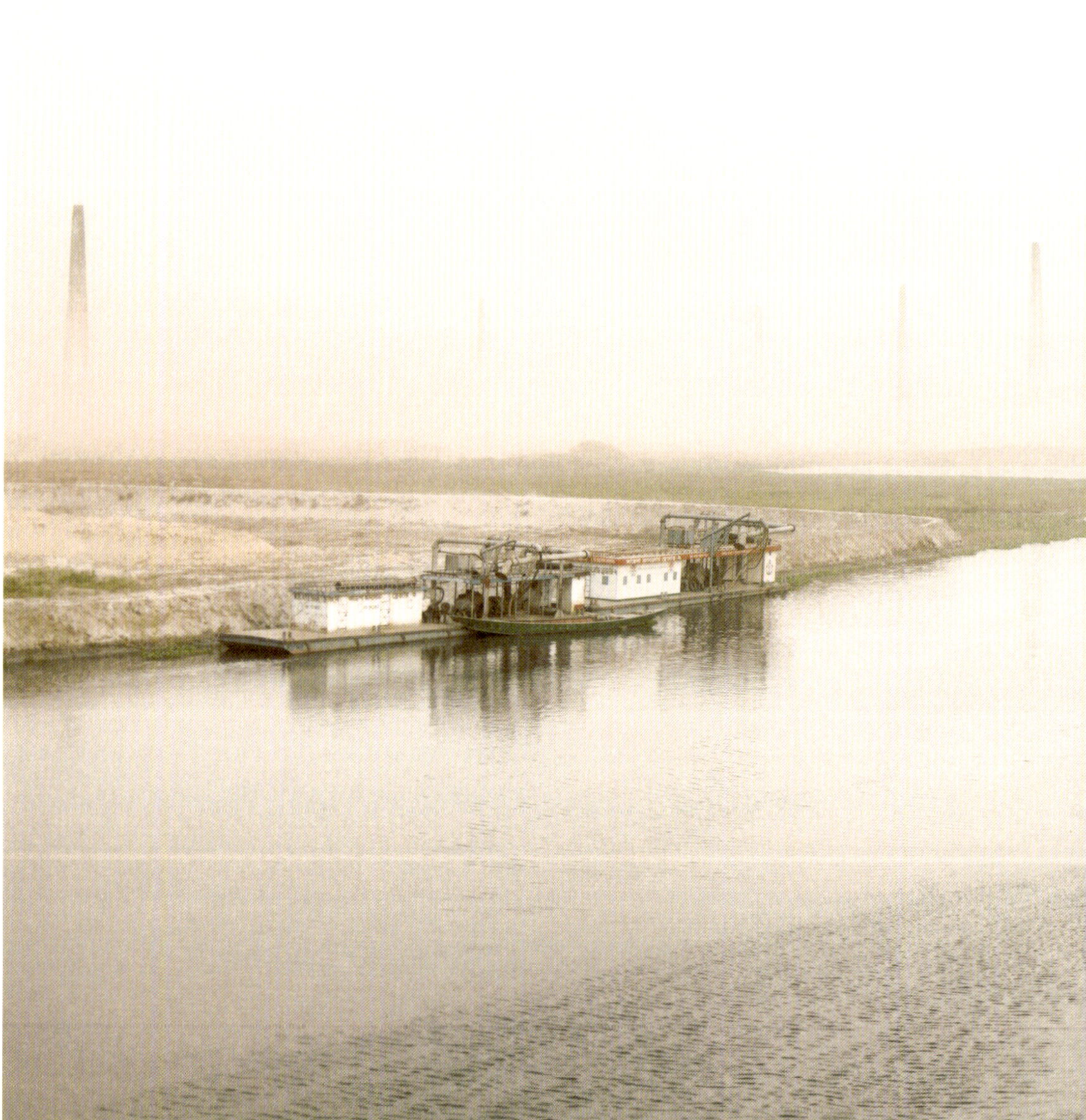

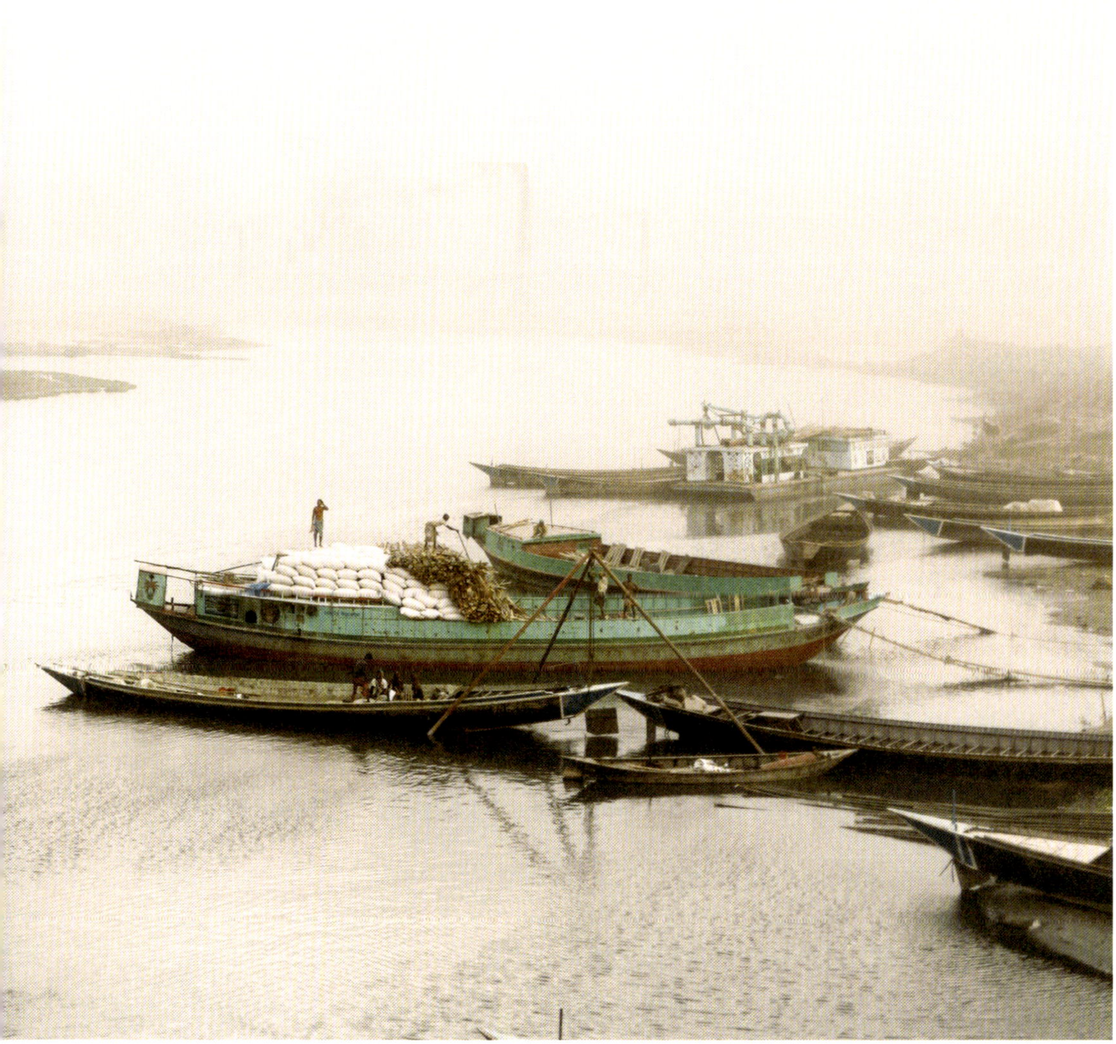

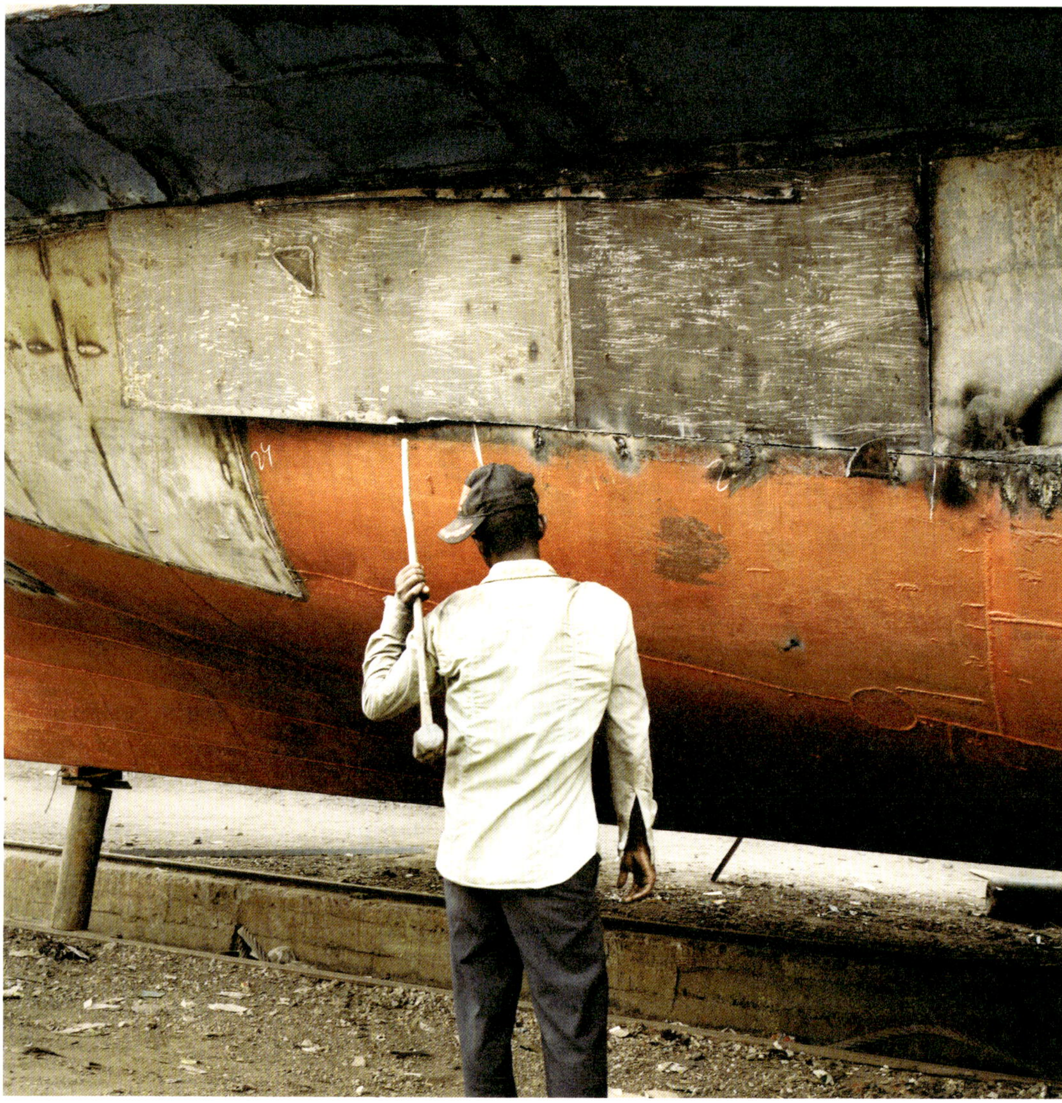

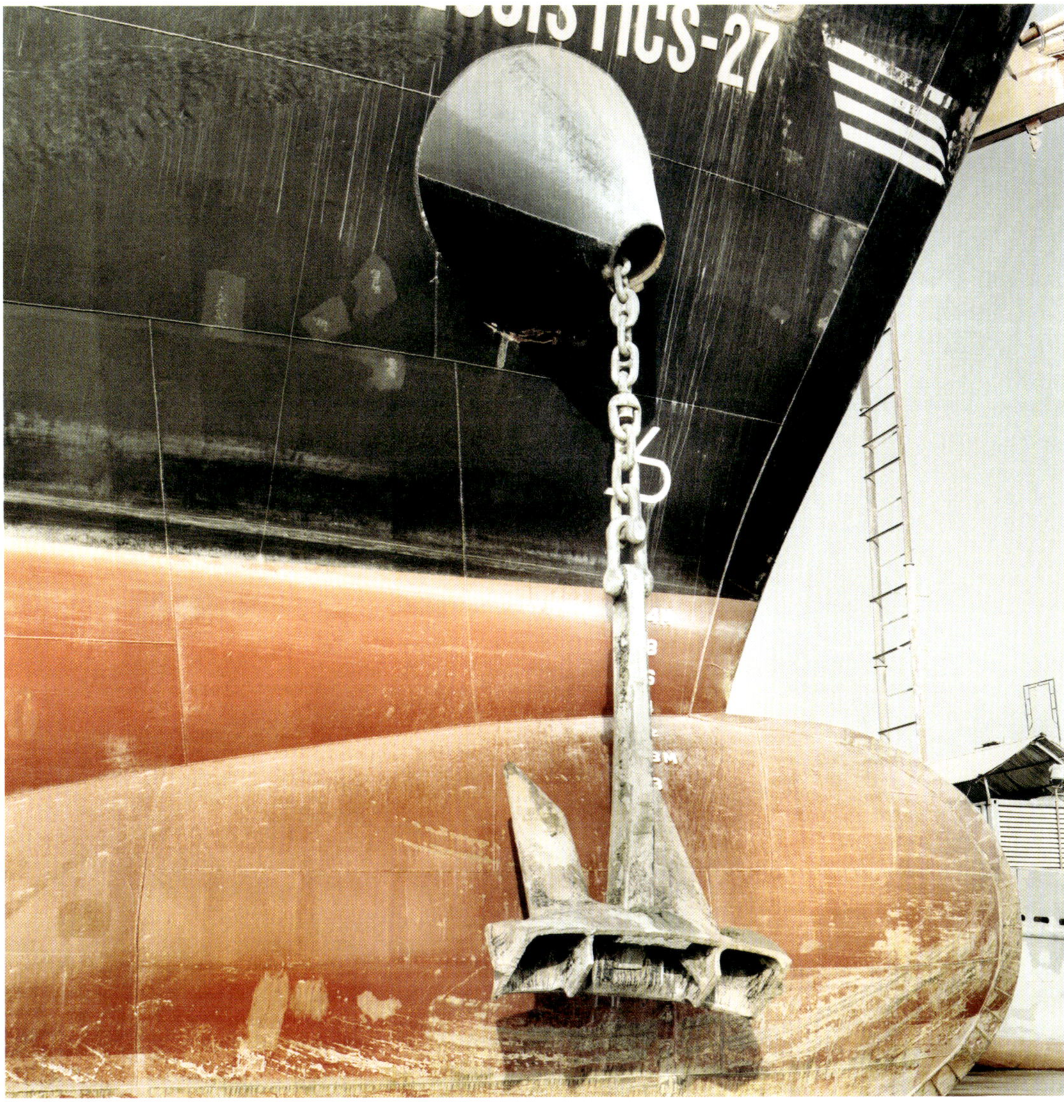

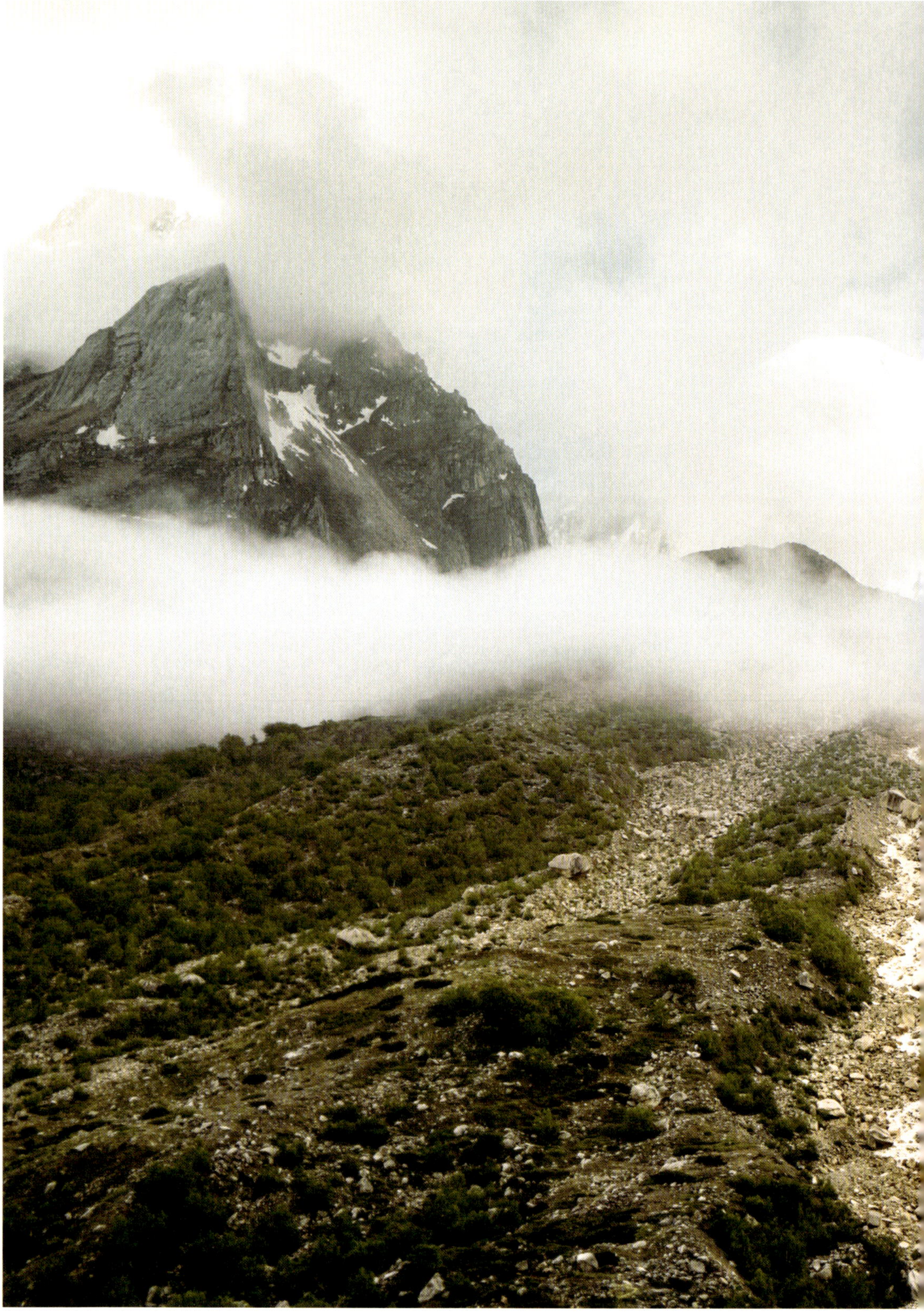

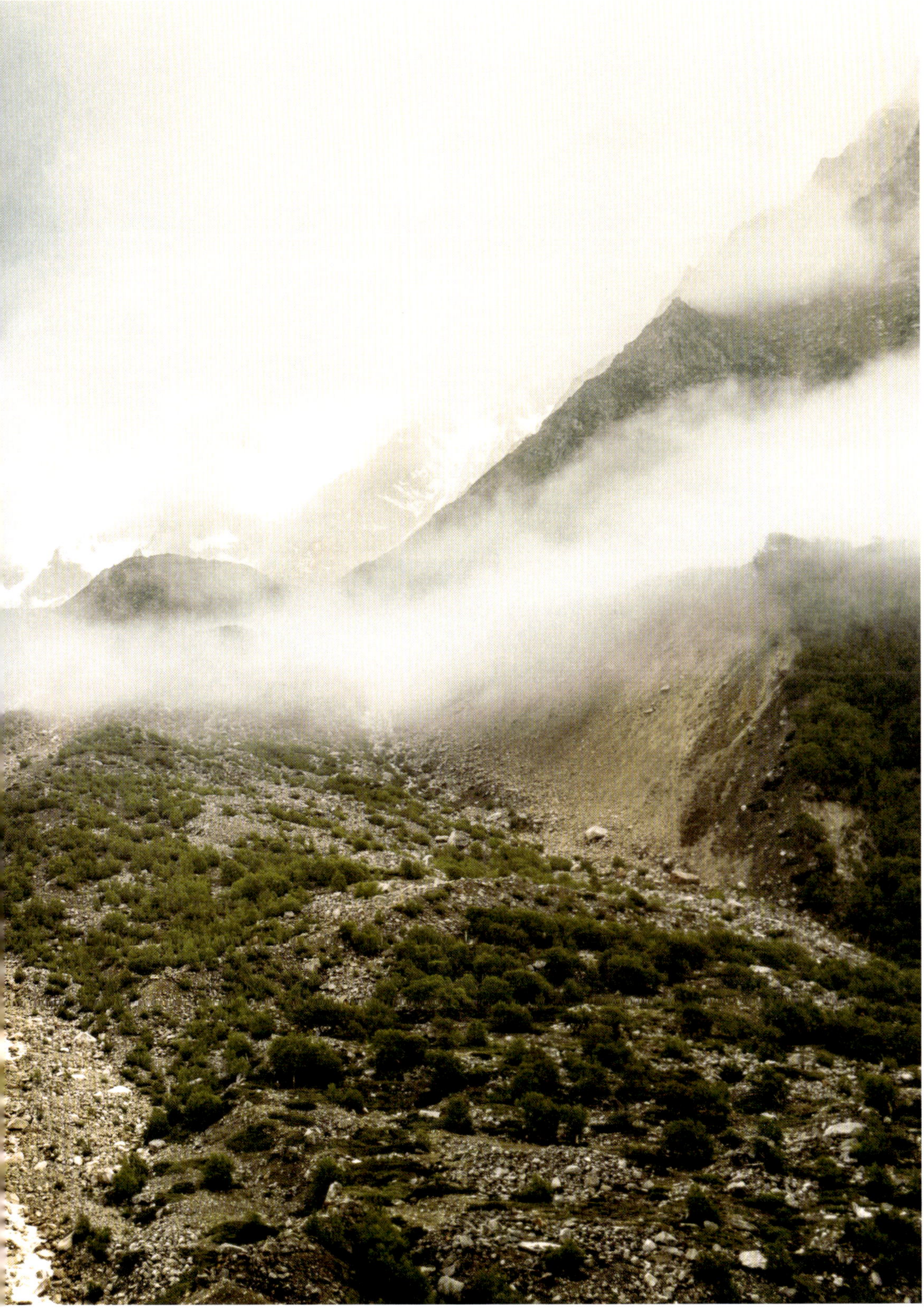

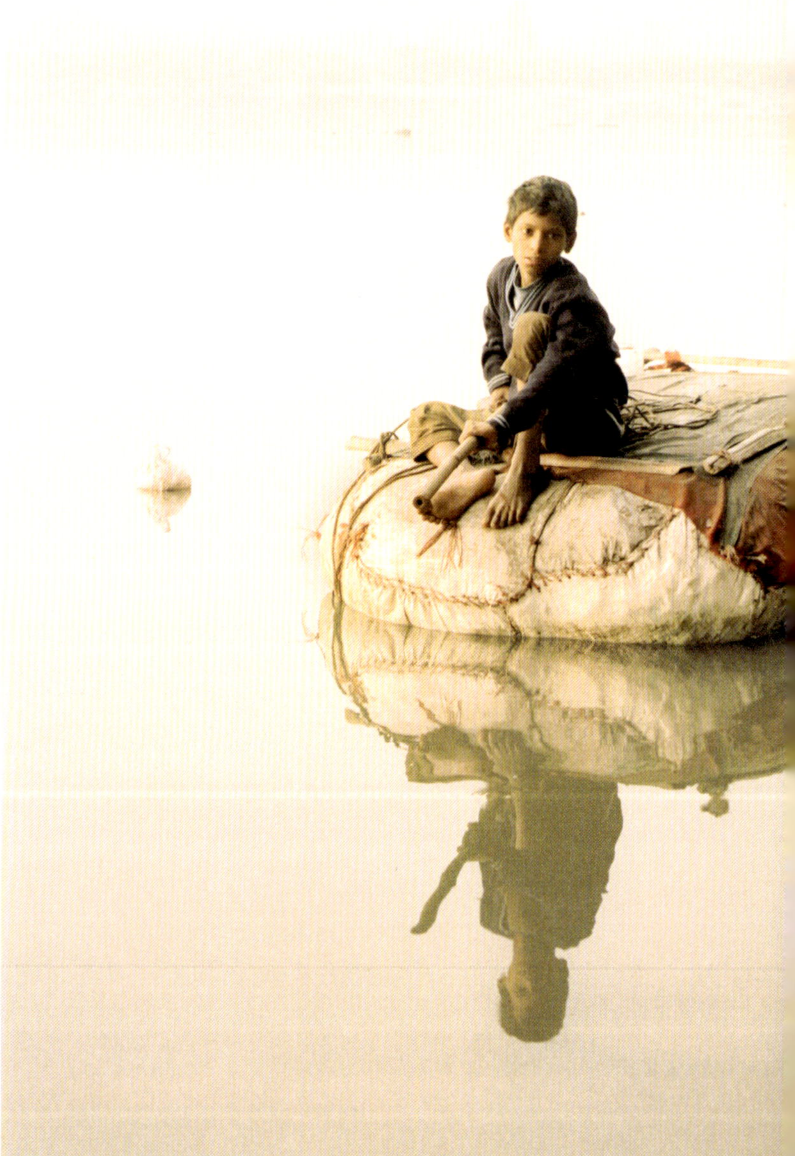

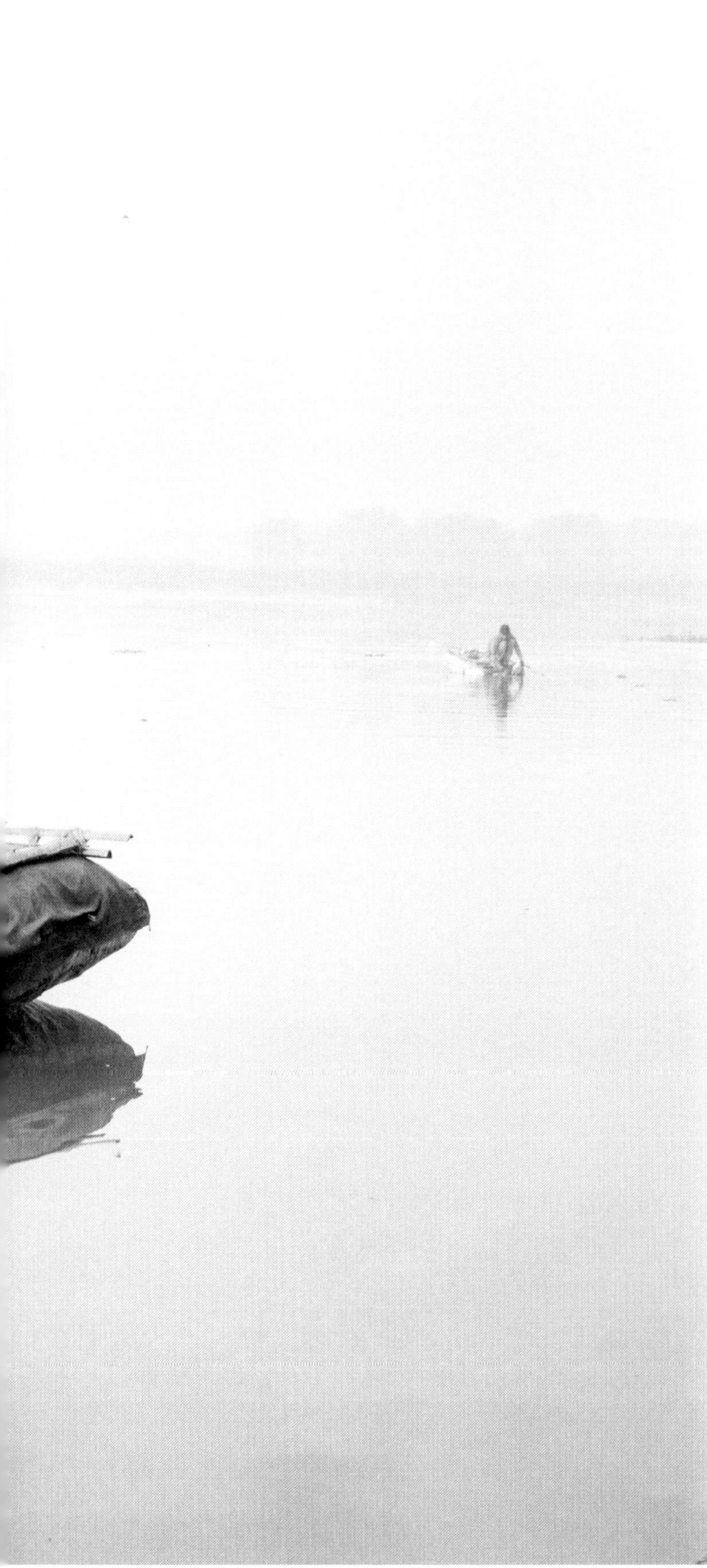

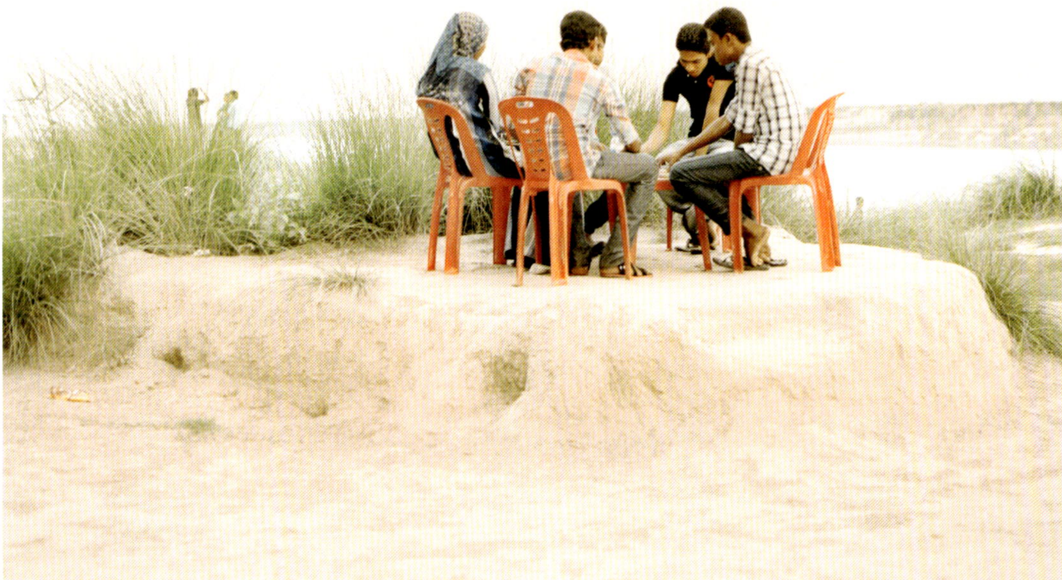

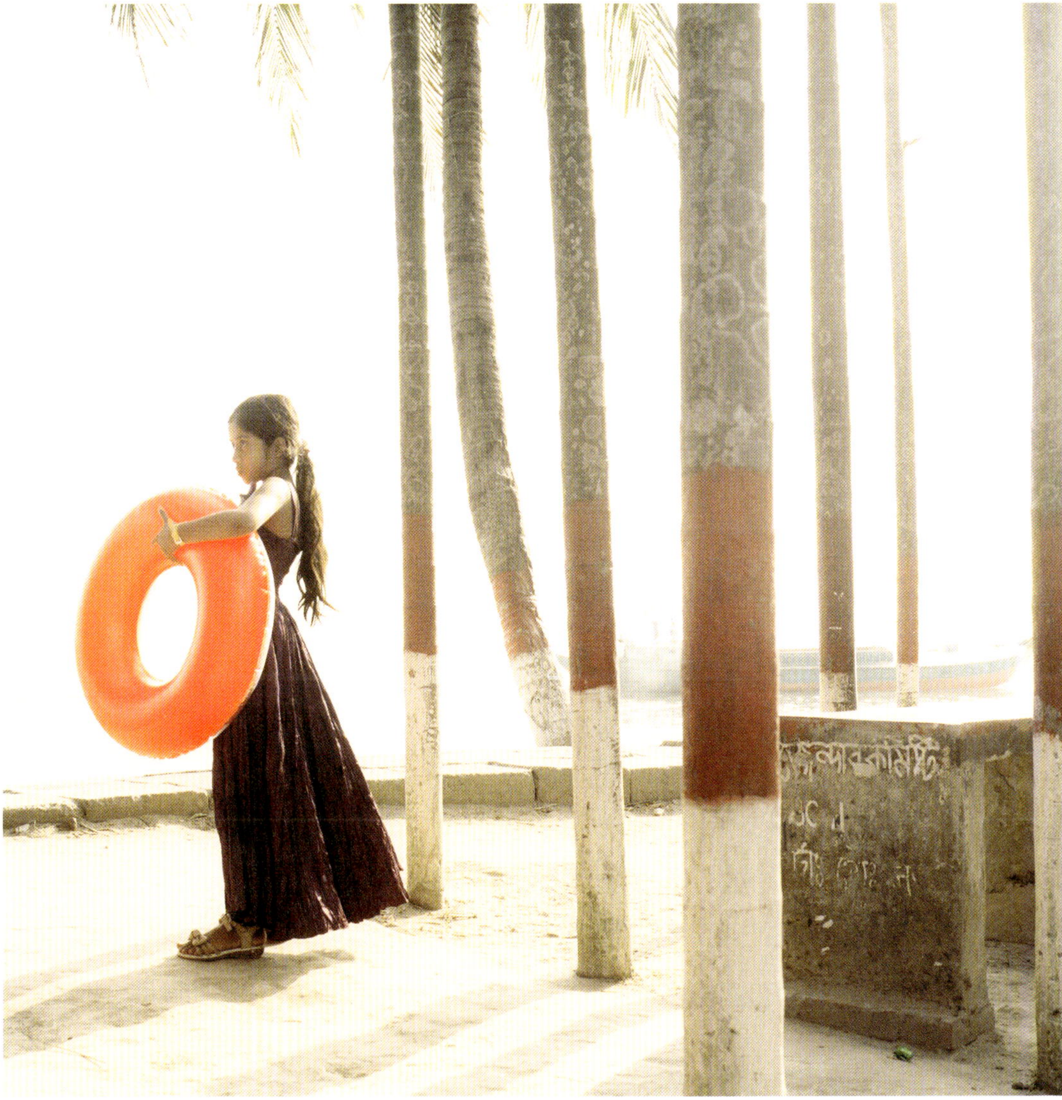

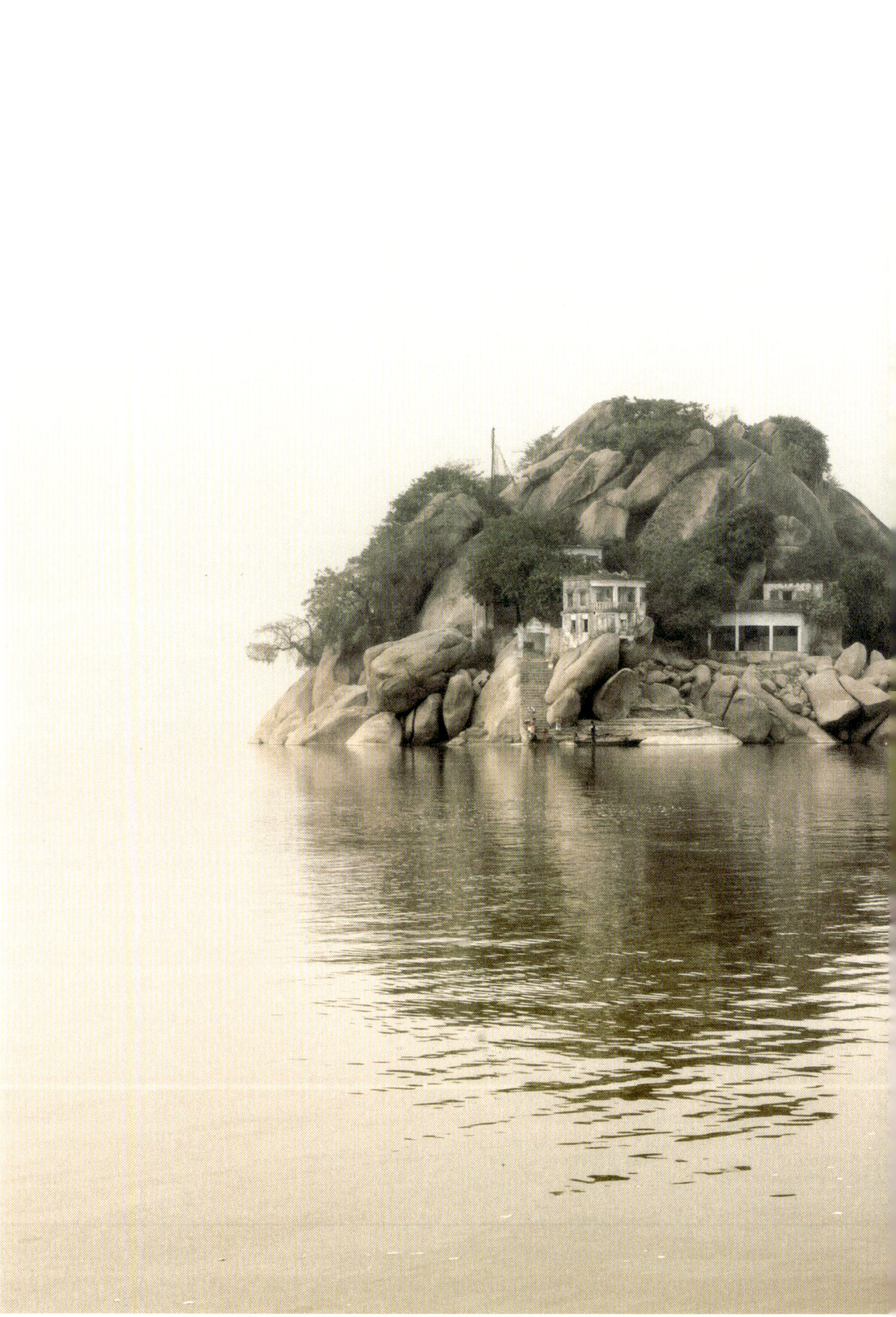

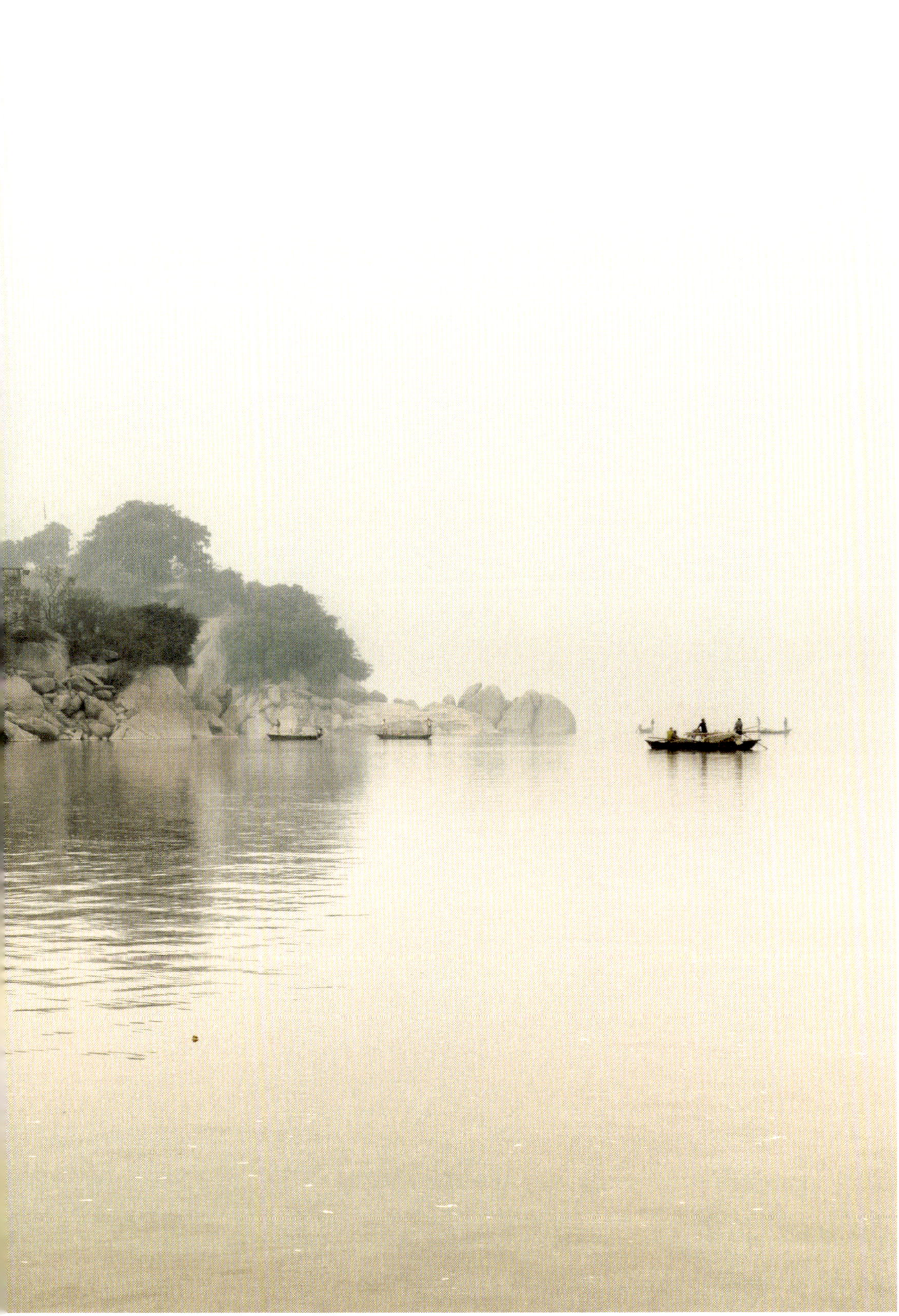

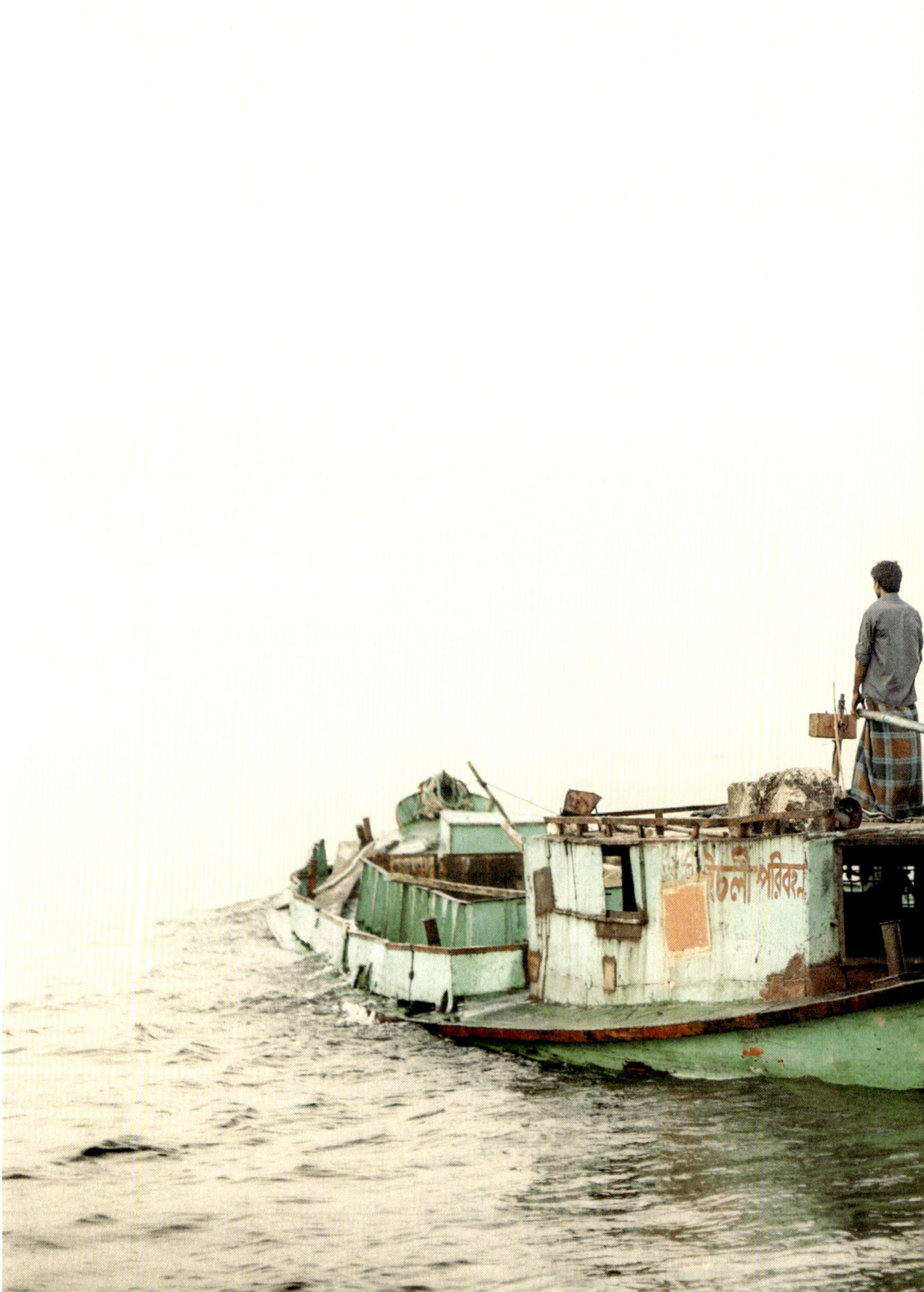

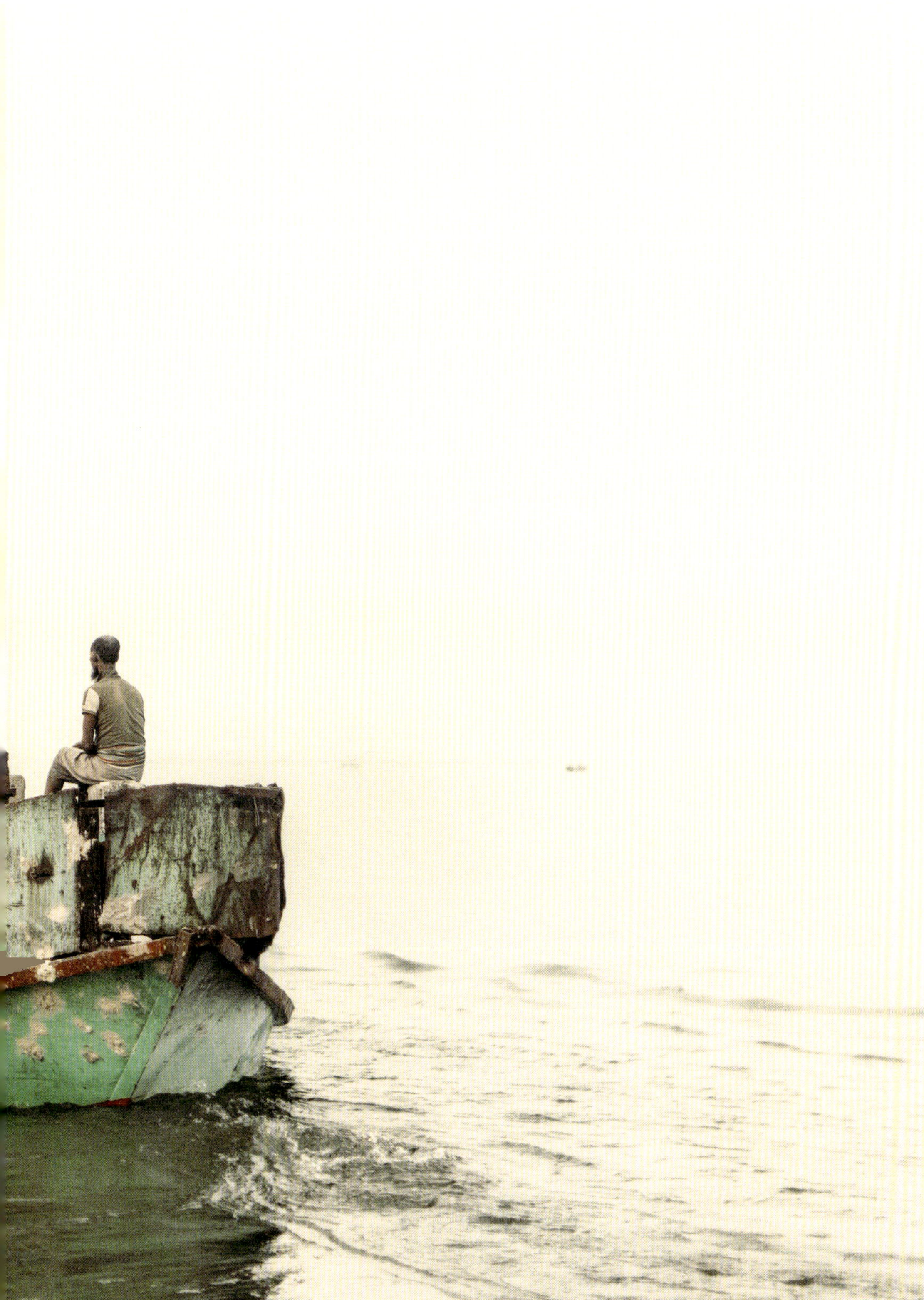

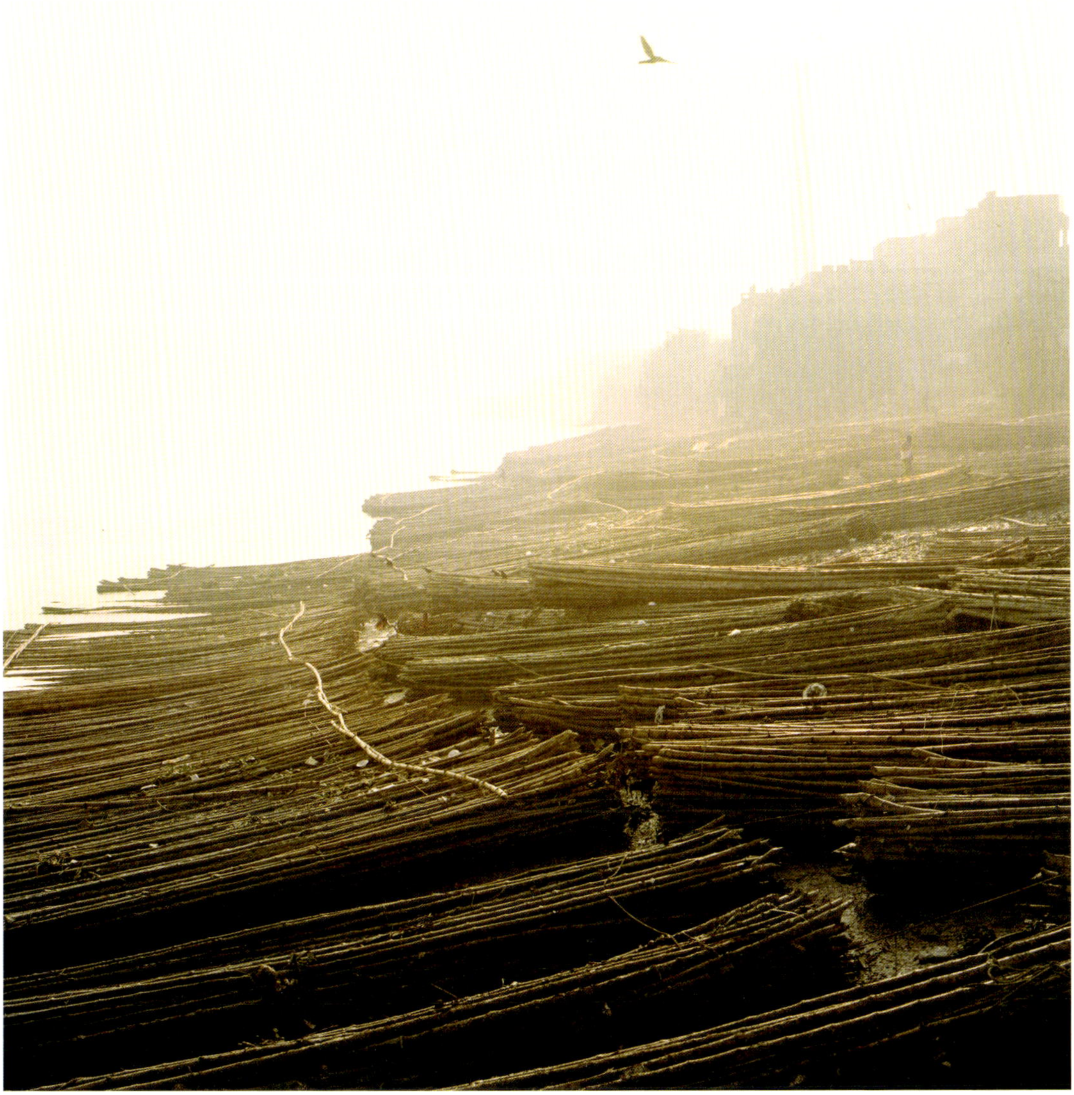

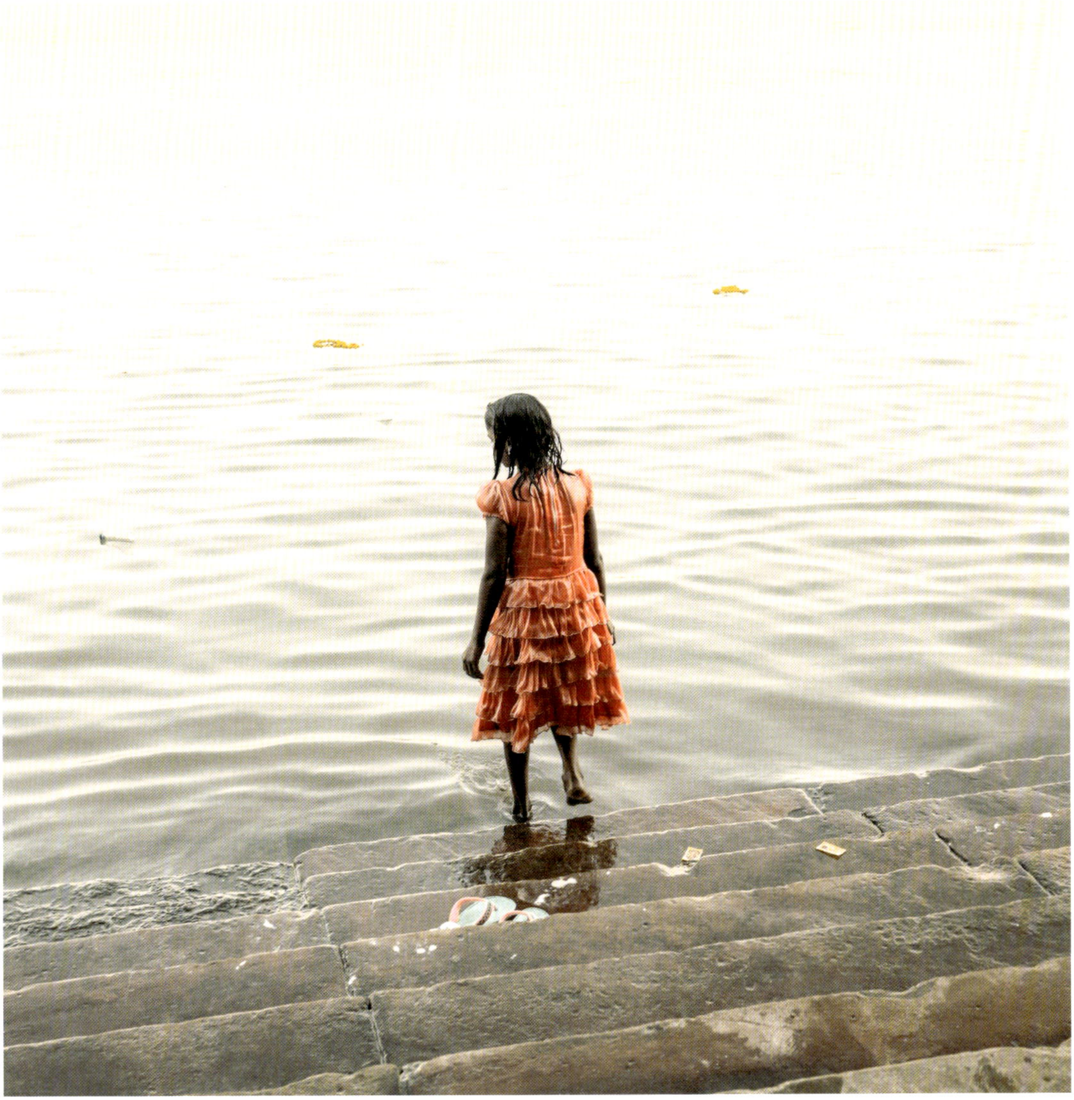

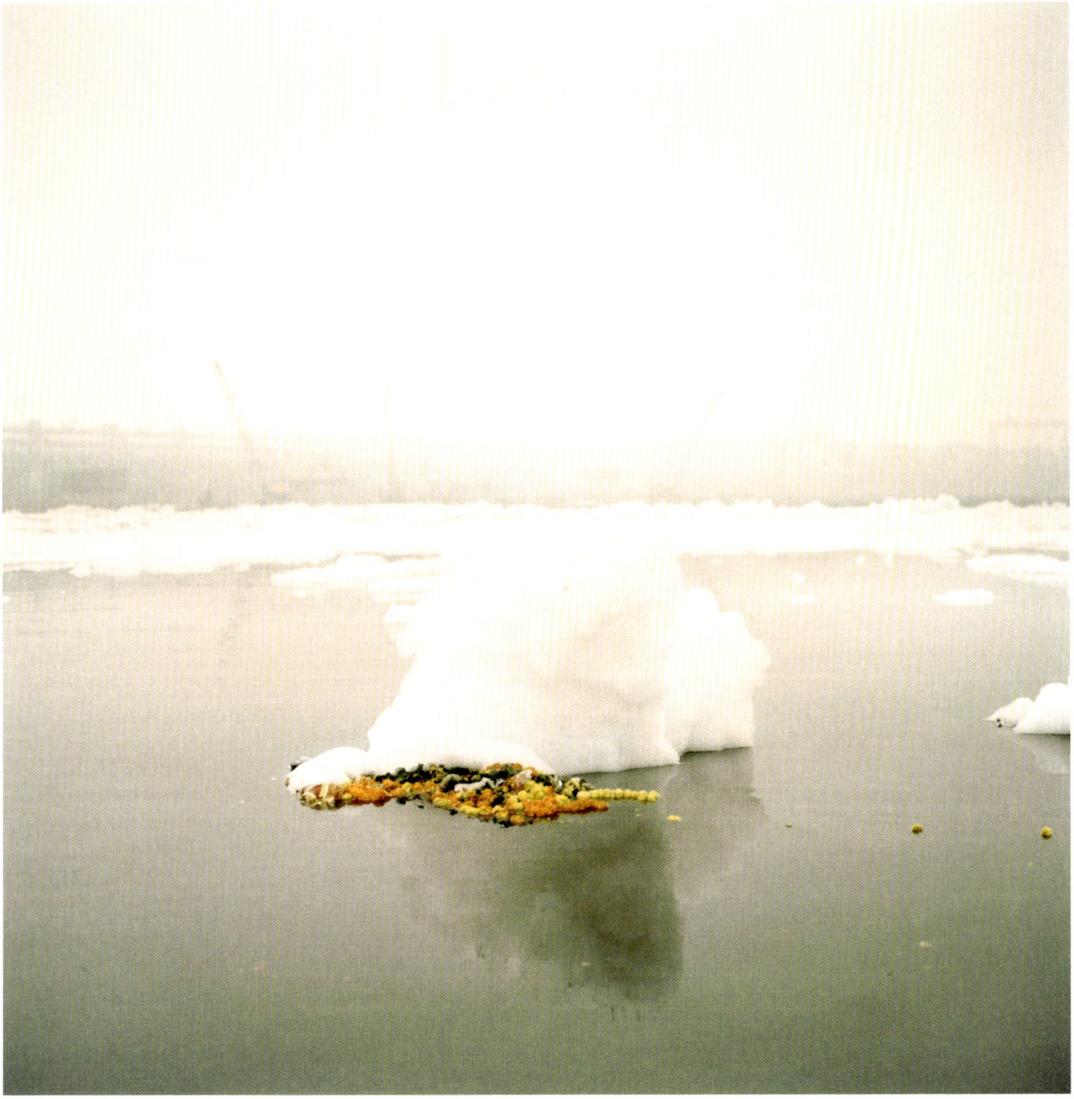

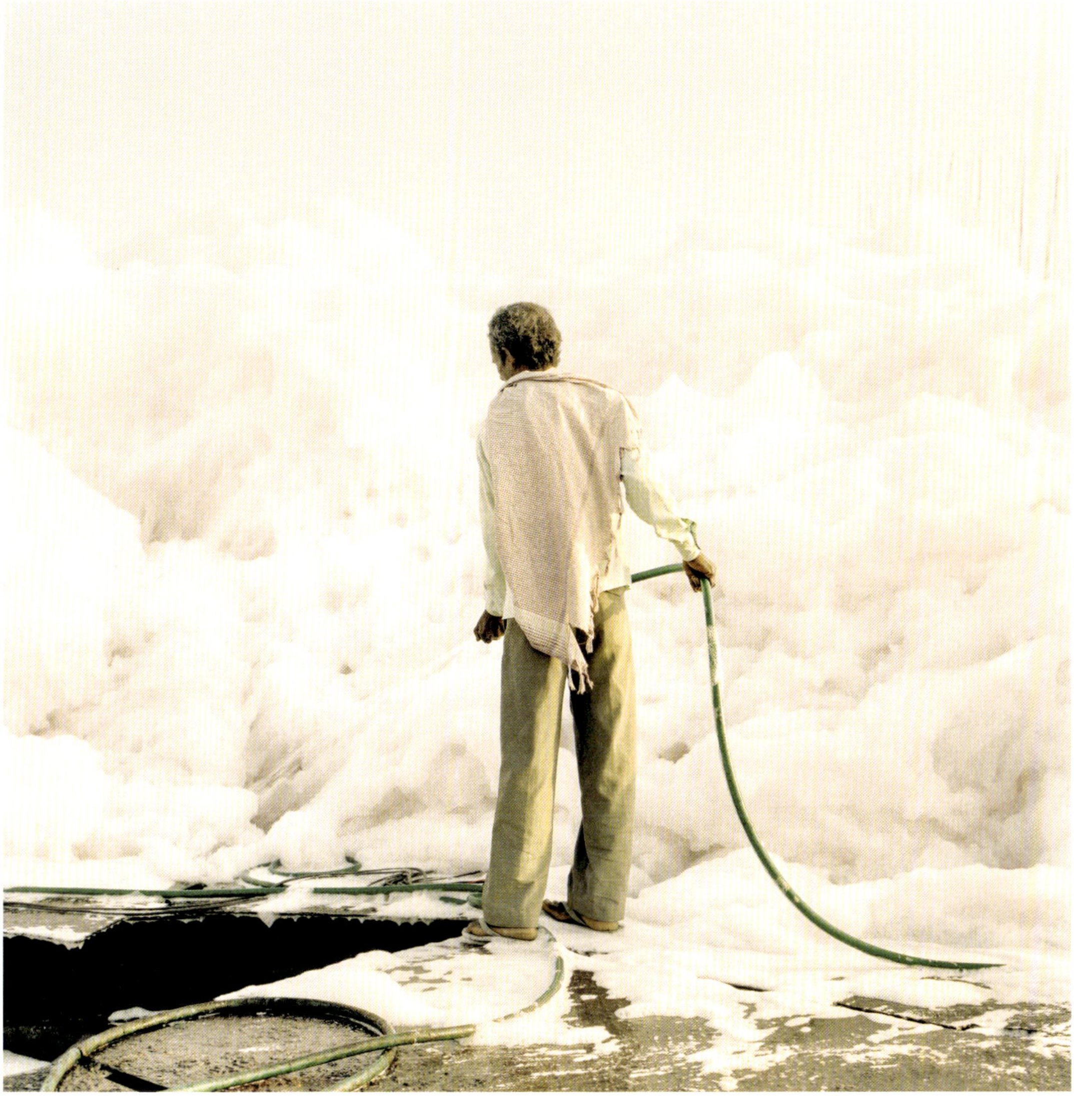

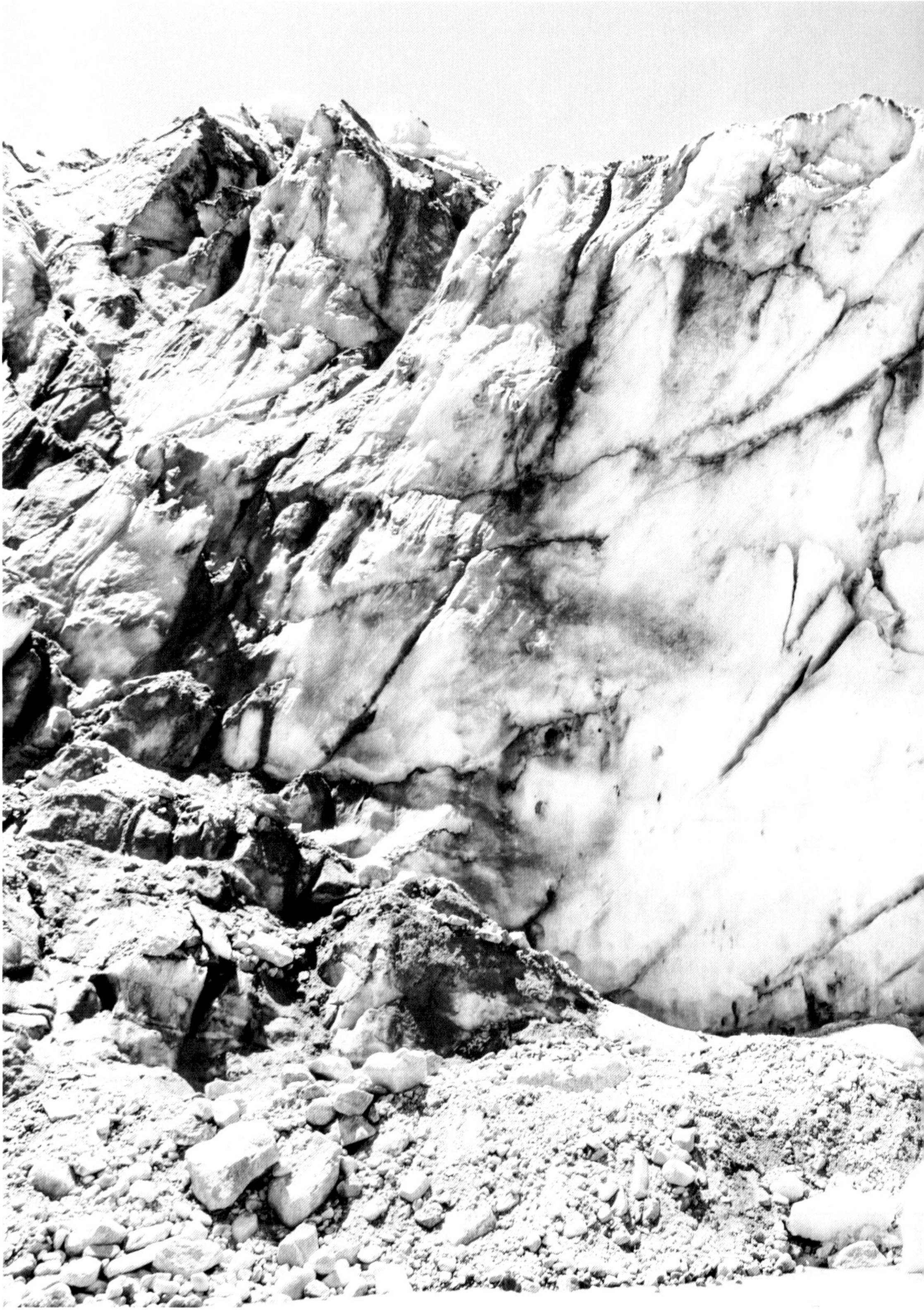

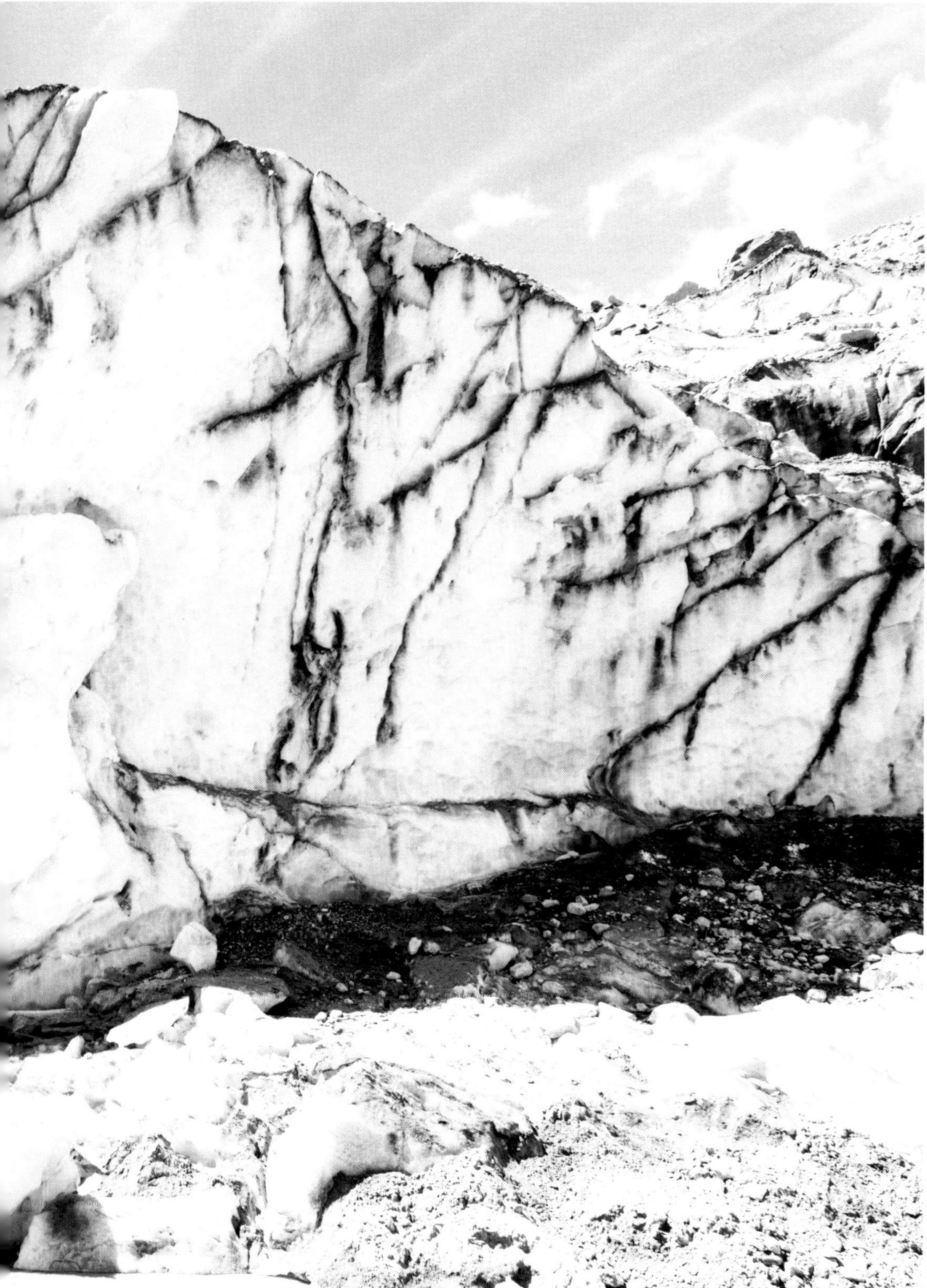

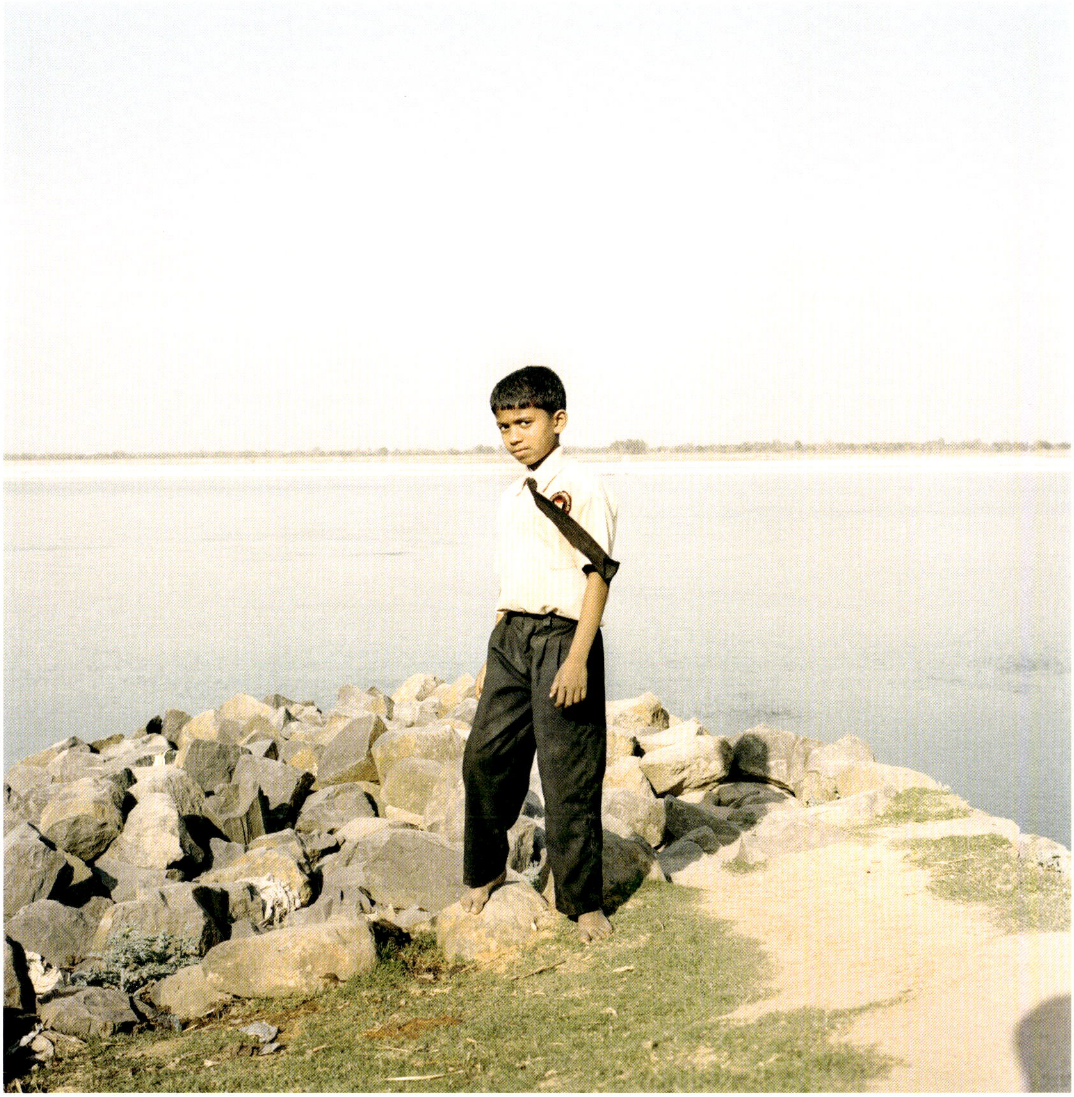

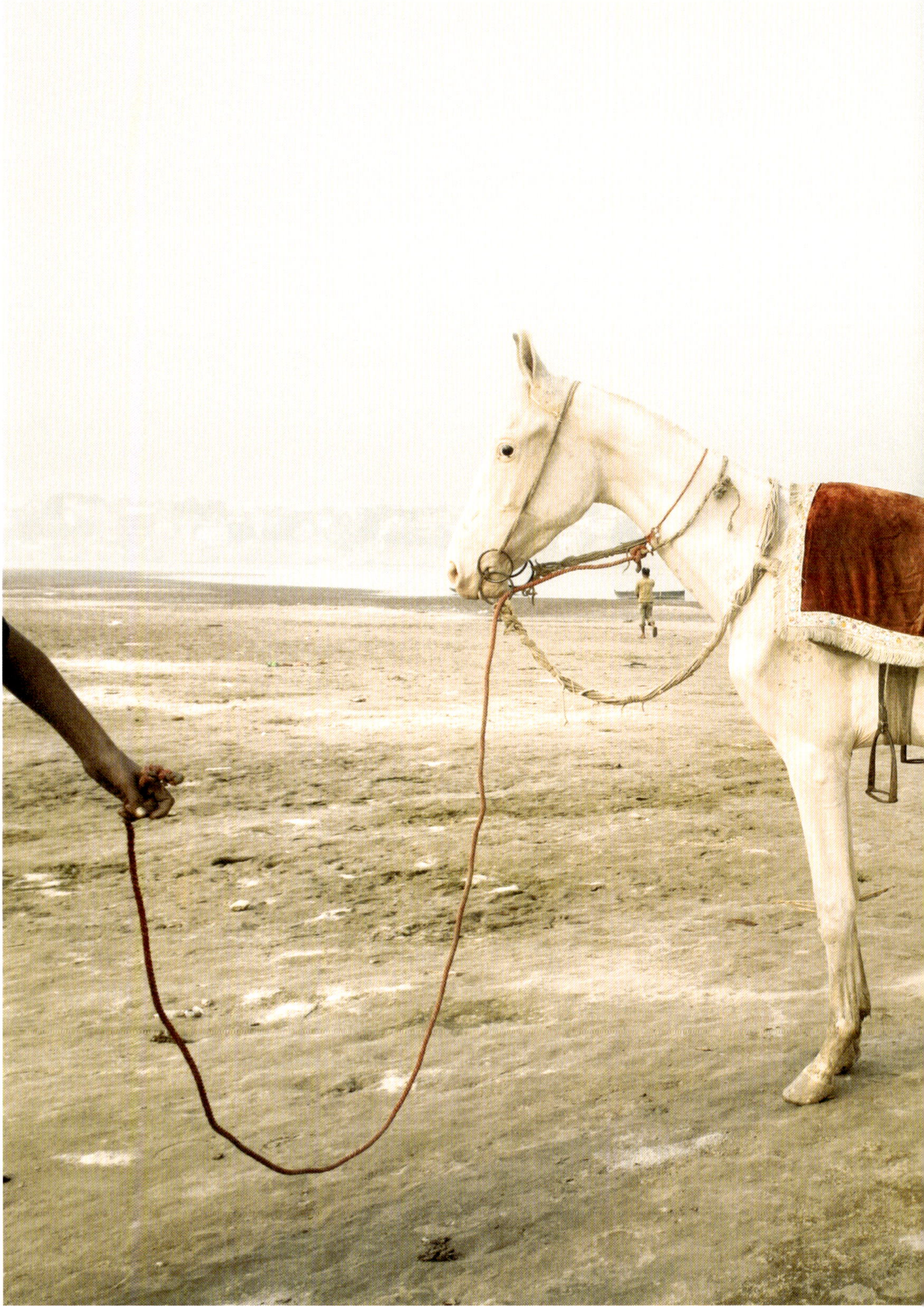

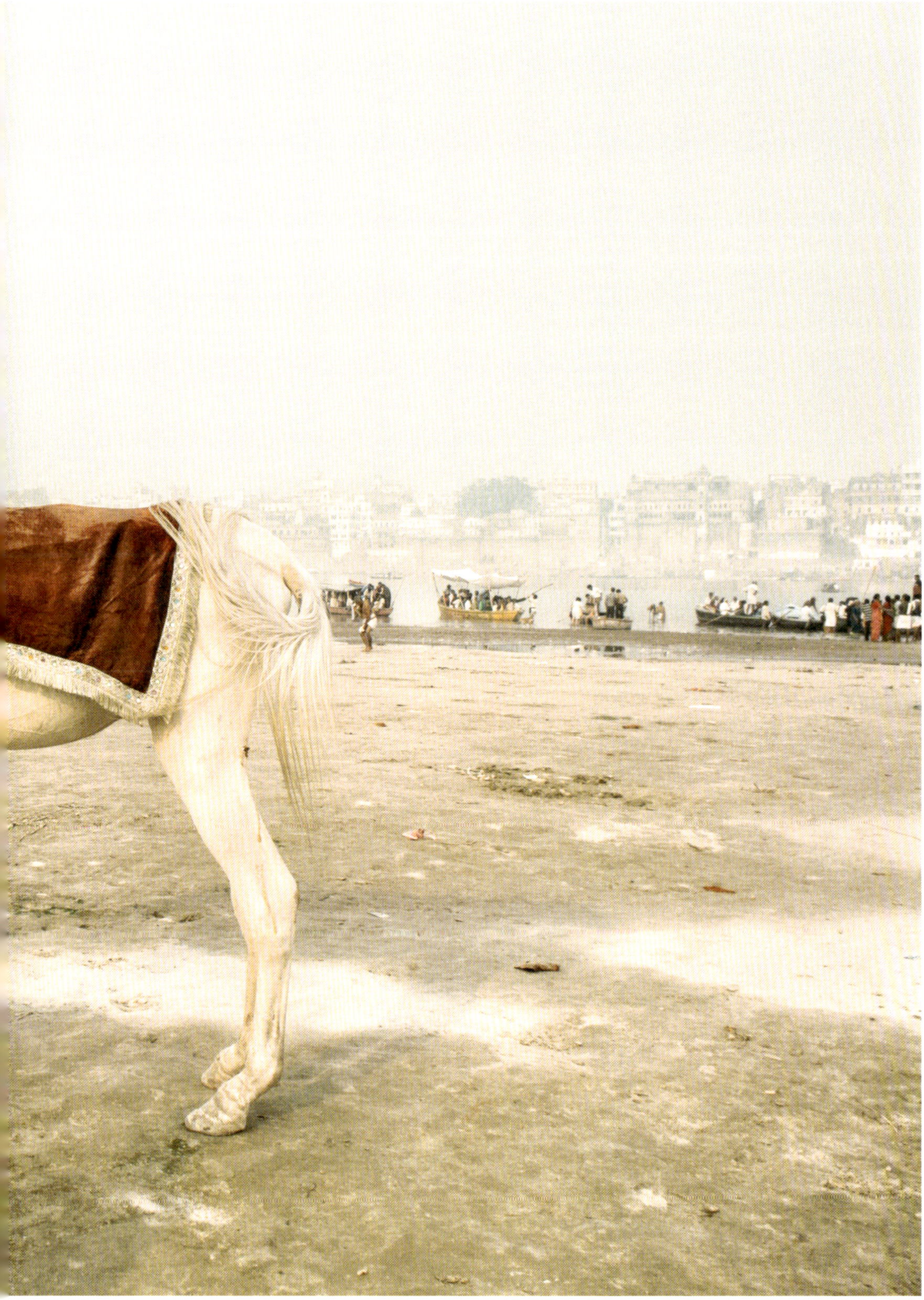

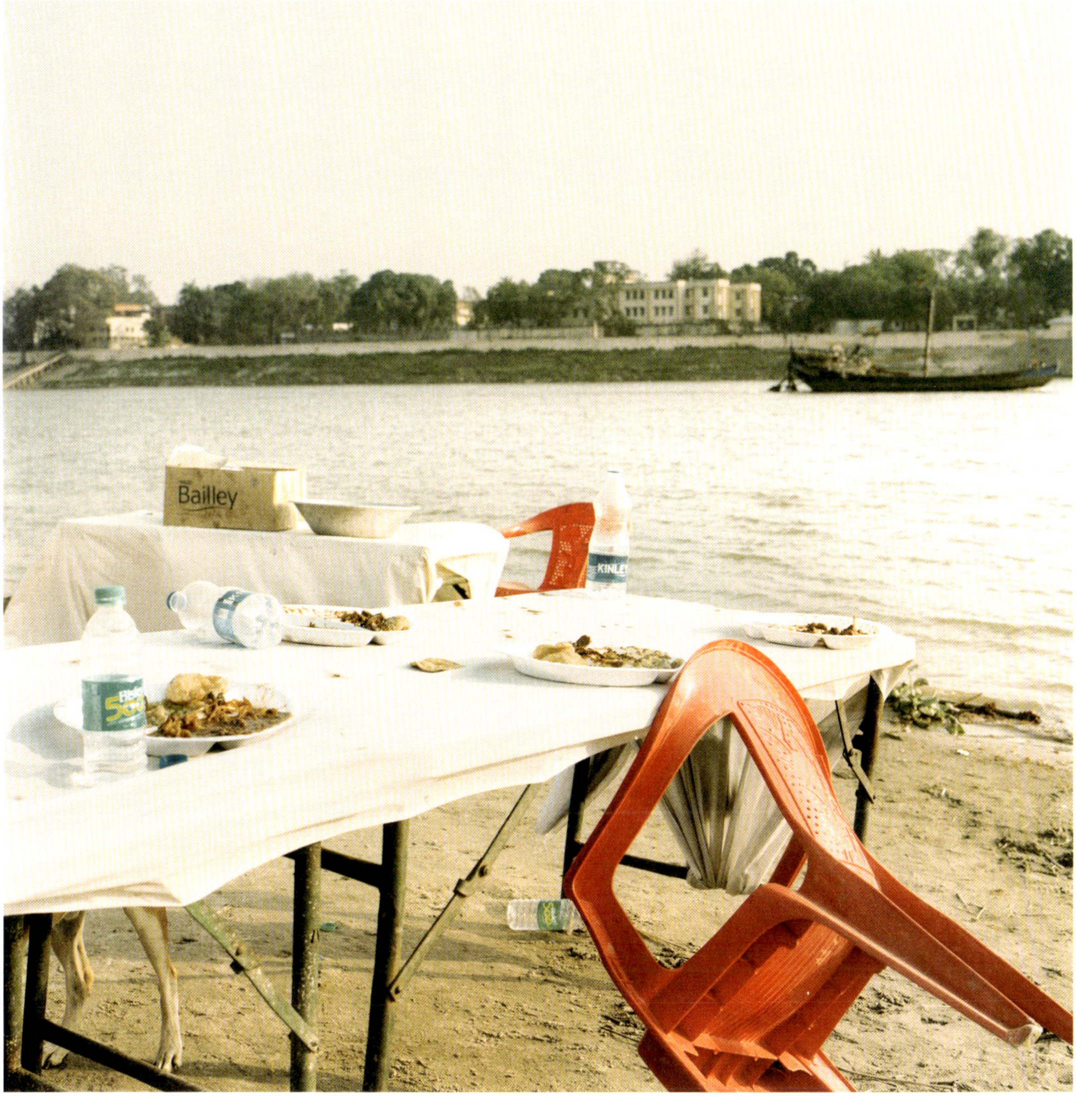
Bailley
KINLEY

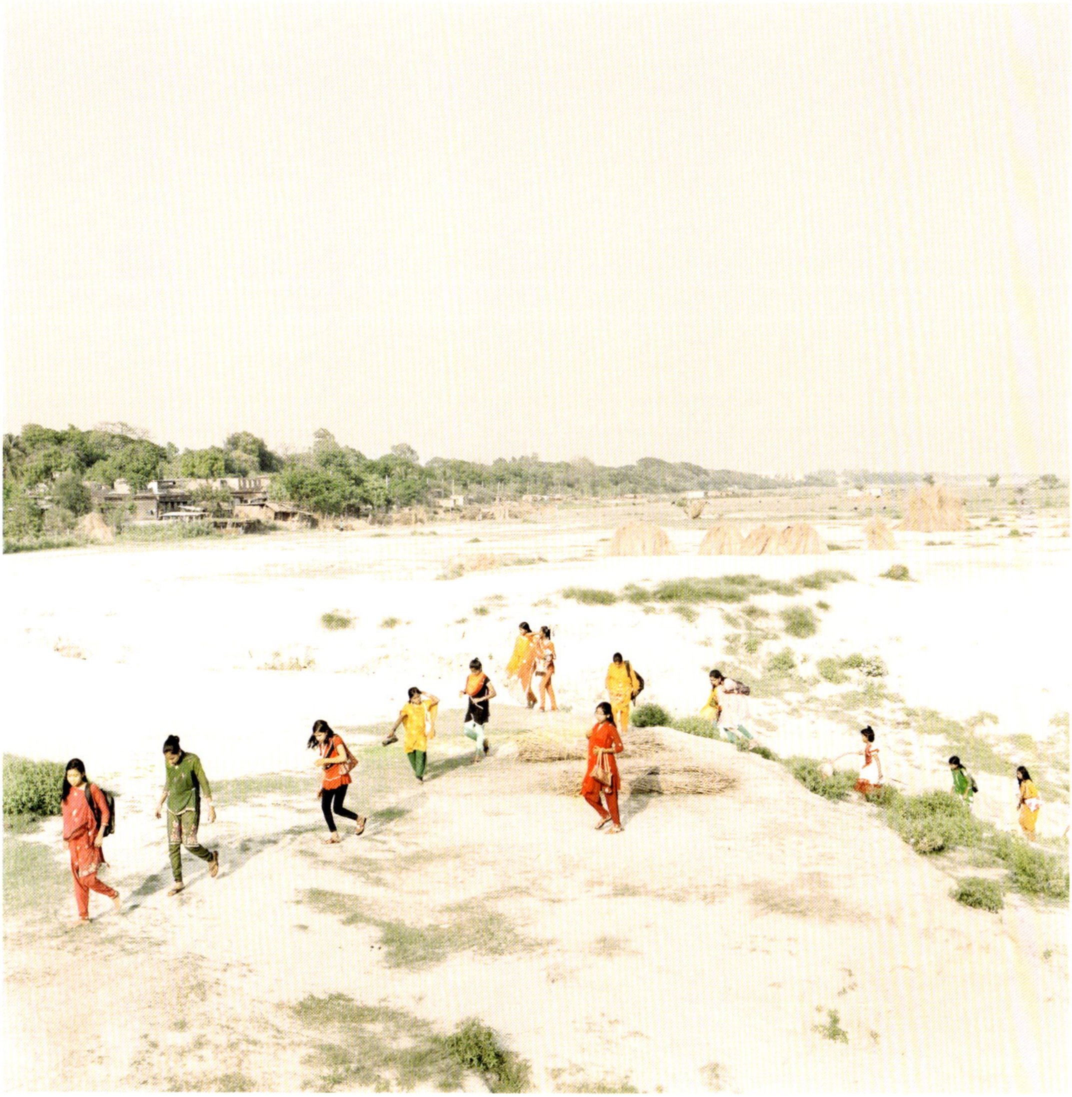

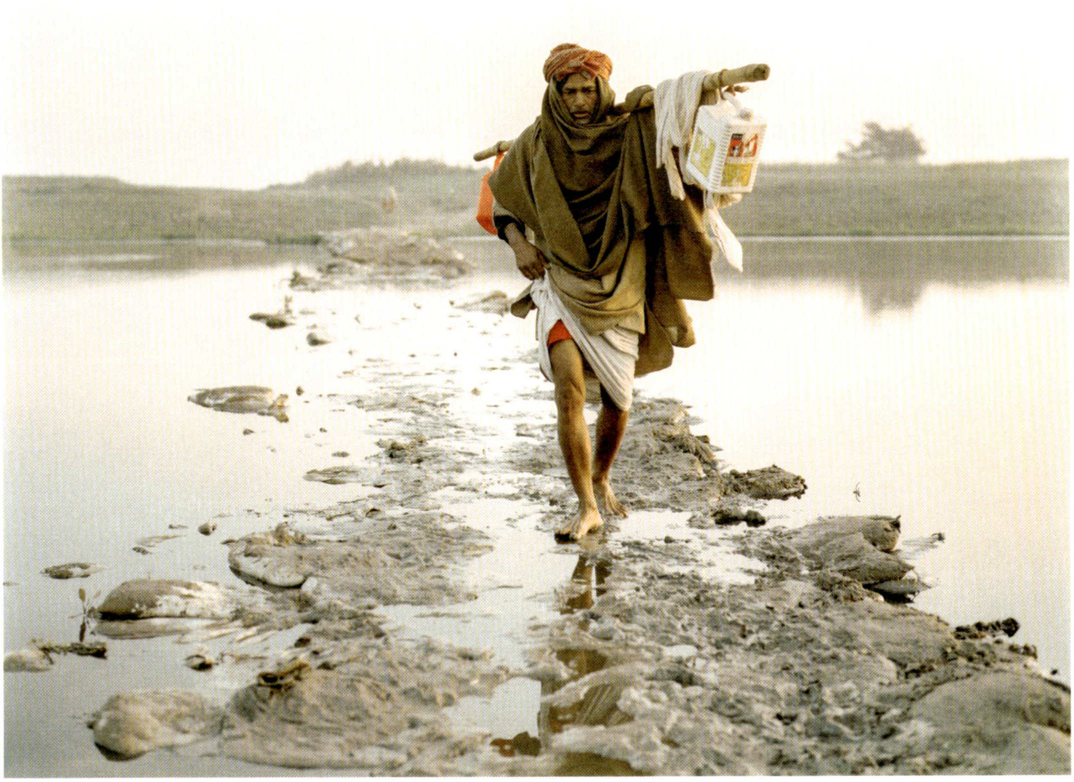

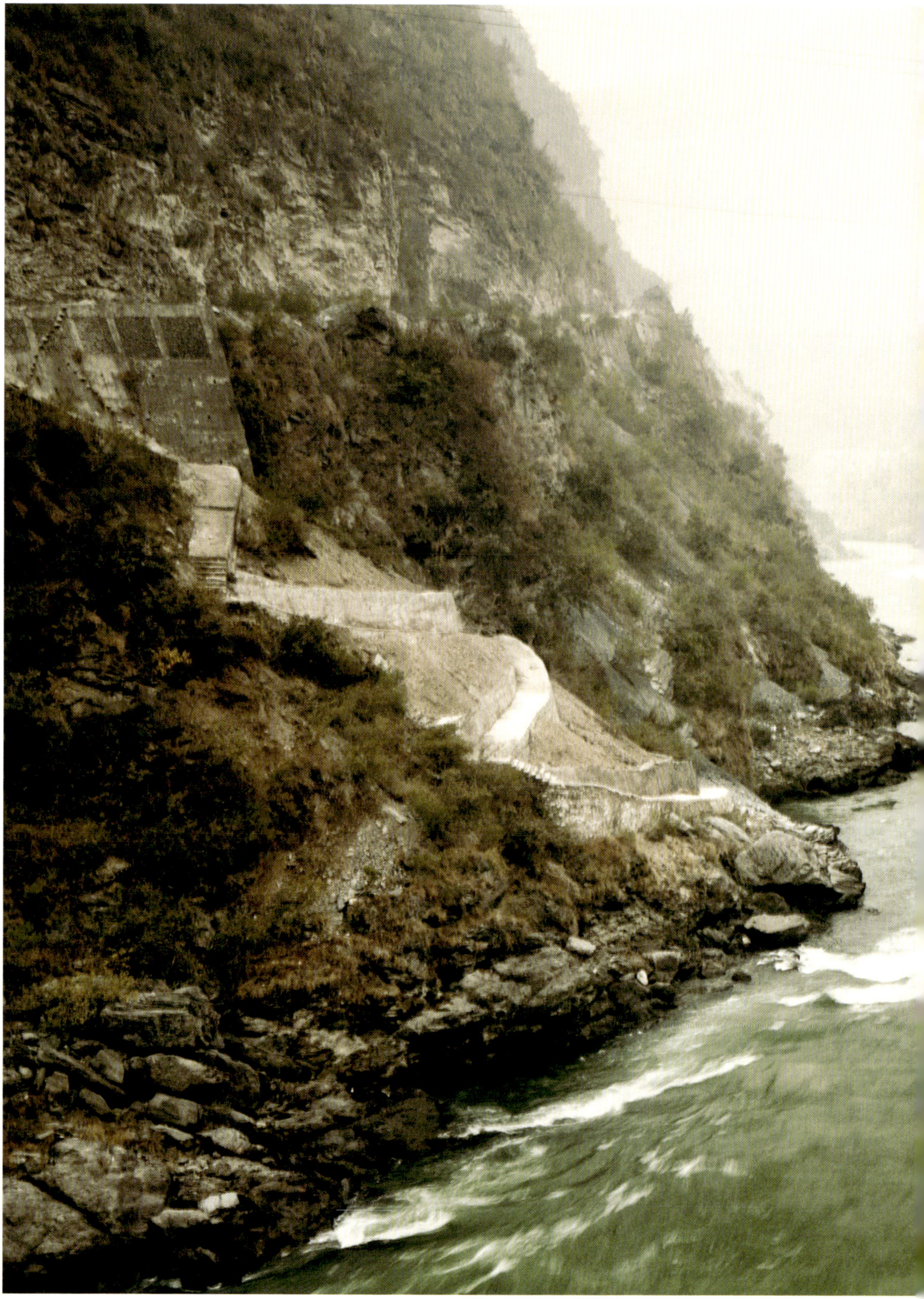

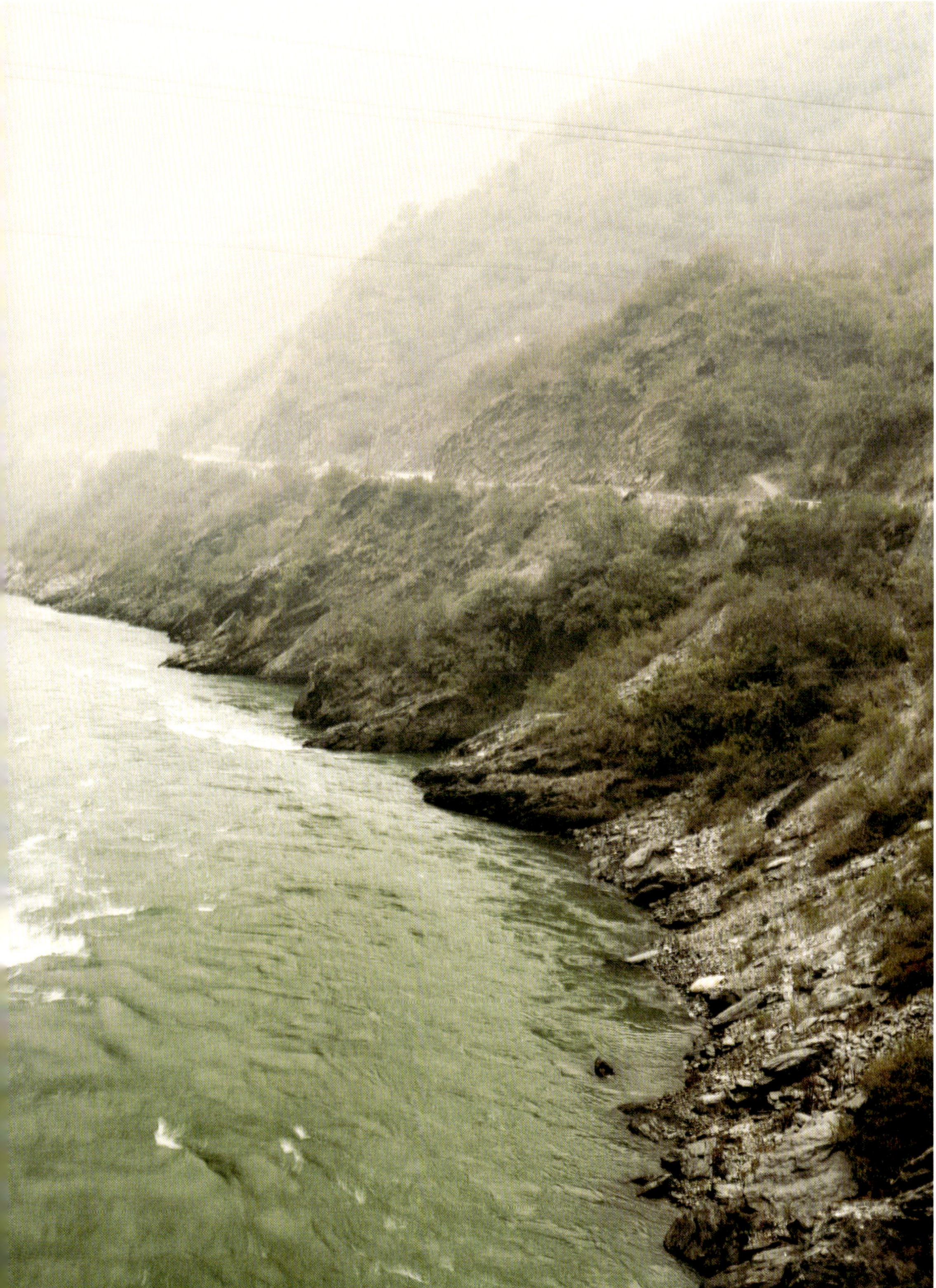

Ma Ganga
India Lives, If Ganga Lives
Vandana Shiva

My home is the land through which the Ganga flows—where the Bhagirathi, the Bhilangana, the Mandakini, the Alaknanda join to form the river which has supported our culture and civilisation, our agriculture and economy from times immemorial. I have spiritually and ecologically experienced her as a Mother—Ma Ganga.

Today, a war has been declared on our sacred mother Ganga, from the Gangotri Glacier where she originates, to its catchments in the Himalaya, through the Ganges basin, till it meets the Indian ocean in the Bay of Bengal.

I started my ecological activism in the 1970s with the Chipko movement —the movement started by women to protect the Himalaya forests in the catchment of the Ganges and her tributaries. Deforestation was a major threat to the catchment of the Ganga in the 1970's. The story of the descent of the Ganga is in fact an ecological story that connects the river to the mountain forests, symbolised as Shiva's hair.

Ganga, whose waves in swarga flow,
Is daughter of the Lord of Snow.
Win Shiva, that his aid be lent,
To hold her in her mid-descent.
For earth alone will never bear
These torrents travelled from the upper air.

My sisters in Chipko reminded the world that timber and profits were not the main products of the forest. Soil, water and pure air are the primary forests.

After the 1978 flood in the Ganga, it became clear that water conservation was the first gift of the Himalayan forests. After nearly a decade of Chipko actions, logging was banned in the high Himalaya in 1981 and the forests are supposed to be managed for conservation, not exploitation.

Climate Change is giving rise to higher temperatures in the Himalaya which in turn is leading to a decline in snowfall and an increase in the rate of melting of the snow. This is threatening the Ganga at its very source, at the Gangotri glacier. From 1935 to 1956 the retreat of the Gangotri glacier was 4.35 metres per year. In the period 1990-1996, it was 28.33 metres per year. The average rate of retreat is currently 20-38 metres per year. If this retreat continues, the Ganga will become a seasonal river, with major ecological and economic consequences for the entire Ganges basin on which most of India depends. This is why we need climate justice for water justice.

In June 2013, climate-change-related extreme weather events, combined with ignorance and greed—ignorance of the ecological systems that hold up the fragile Himalayas, and greed to profit from the exploitation of the land and water resources of the Himalaya—led to flooding in the Kedarnath Valley. Villages, schools, roads and bridges were washed away. Thousands disappeared in the floods.

Our region in the Himalaya is called 'Dev Bhoomi'—the Divine and Sacred land. Today, it has been defined as 'Urja Pradesh'—the land of hydroelectric power. Planners do not see our rivers as rivers of life. They see them instead as sources of 20,000 megawatts of hydro power. In 1916, in his book *Garhwal, Ancient and Modern*, Rai Patiram Bahadur wrote: 'We may say that there is no country in the world of the dimension of Garhwal which has so many rivers as a traveller will find in this land. The district has sixty rivers of different size, besides these, there are rivulets, rills, springs and fountains in hundreds, showing that nature has been especially bountiful to this land in the matter of its water supply.'

This idyllic picture no longer exists today. The Ganga's tributaries are threatened by dams and diversions in the upper reaches. The Tehri dam has been an unmitigated disaster. The 260.5 metre-high Tehri dam has been built at Tehri on the confluence of the Bhagirathi and Bhilangana. It submerged the ancient capital of Tehri Garhwal, destroyed the lush and fertile fields of Bhilangana and Bhagirathi valleys and displaced 100,000 people from 125 villages, of which thirty-three were completely submerged. Mooni Devi, who lives at water level, says 'This used to be such a great place with great farms, the dam builders have turned us all into beggars.' But the displacement due to the dam continues. One hundred new landslides have been triggered by the dam threatening another 100,000 people. In the heavy monsoon of 2010, the disasters intensified.

A chain of hydroelectric projects have stopped the *aviral* (uninterrupted) flow of Ganga. In many stretches, the Ganga runs dry. The government of India has been proposing hydro-electric projects on Loharinag Pala, Pala Maneri and Bhaironghati on Bhagirathi to tap their hydro-power potential. In addition to the already built Tehri Dam and Maneri Bhali II Dam, a series of dams are planned between Gangotri and Uttarkashi on the river Bhagirathi.

In 2008, our teacher and friend, Professor G.D. Agarwal, a former professor of IIT Kanpur where I attended summer schools as a physics student, undertook a fast into death at the age of seventy-six to stop the string of dams including the 600 megawatts Loharinag Pala being built by the Natural Thermal Power Corporation. Under this proposal, the Ganga would be put into a 17 kilometres tunnel to generate electricity. Other planned dams on the Bhagirathi included the 480 megawatts Pala Maneri and the 381 megawatts Bharan Ghati. On 14 January 2009, Prof. Agarwal undertook a fast again because the government failed to stop the dam. After continued fasts by Prof. Agarwal, the Lohari Nappala dam was stopped.

Announcing the suspension of the dam projects on the Bhagirathi, the Union Minister of Environment, Jairam Ramesh, stated: 'I have said in Parliament that India is a civilisation of rivers, that it should not become a land of tunnels... There are no two opinions. There is just one mass opinion that the projects proposed on the river Bhagirathi, named Pala Maneri and Bhaironghate projects will not be entertained any further by the government.'

Professor Agarwal, also known as Swami Gyan Swaroop Sanand, died on 11 October 2018 at the age of eighty-six, after 111 days of fast unto death for the conservation of mother river Ganga. His demands of the government included the cessation of four under-construction hydropower projects on the Ganga and putting an end to tree felling and mining practices in the Ganga river bed.

Other saints have joined the *tapasya* (penance) to defend Ganga Ma. A 26 year-old South Indian Brahmachari Atmabodhanandji of Matri Sadan Haridwar also began a fast unto death seeking fulfilment of the same demands. He had completed more than sixty days at the time of writing. Sant Gopal Das remains missing after having undertaken a fast for the Ganga for 150 days.

In the plains a big threat to the Ganga and Yamuna is pollution—from both industry and sewage. And even as billions are poured into cleaning the Ganga and Yamuna through their respective Action Plans, the pollution of our sacred river increases due to a combination of corruption and inappropriate technologies.

Industrialisation and urbanisation have turned our sacred rivers into sinks for pollutants. The Yamuna is clean before entering Delhi. In twenty-two kilometres of its journey through Delhi, it picks up 70% of all the pollution of the river in its total length. All that the Action Plans have done is to set up centralised Sewage Treatment Plants (STPs) that do not work, and 70% of all sewage is dumped untreated into the river. The river dies because of pollution; the land dies because it is deprived of rich nutrients. As Sunderlal Bahuguna reminded me, Gandhi called this 'golden manure.' Intelligent zero-waste sewage treatment systems like those evolved in IIT Kanpur by Dr. Vinod Tare would both clean the Ganga and fertilise the soil. We would not be wasting Rs. 130,000 crores (one crore denotes ten million rupees) on fertiliser subsidies and thousands of crores on river action plans. Organic farming can be a major action for cleaning the Ganga.

The final threat to the Ganga is privatisation. Privatisation of water reduces water to a commodity, turning giant corporations into owners and sellers of water, and ordinary citizens into buyers and consumers. The role of citizens and communities as conservers and caretakers is destroyed. The human right to water, which was recognised by the UN in April 2010, is undermined. That is why, when the Ganges water which has been brought to Delhi from Tehri was being privatised to Suez through a World Bank project, we built a Citizens Alliance for Water Democracy and told the World Bank and the Delhi Government that our 'Mother Ganga is not for sale.' The World Bank project was then withdrawn and the privatisation stopped.

In August 2002, people across the country, together with the water activist Oscar Olivera who led the movement against Bolivia's water privatisation, joined in solidarity to stop the privatisation of Mother Ganga at Har Ki Pauri in Haridwar and gave a rallying cry through the Haridwar declaration:

'Mother Ganga Is Not for Sale'

Today, the 8th of August 2002, on the eve of the 60th Anniversary of the 'Quit India Movement,' we all have gathered here to pledge that: We will never let the river Ganga to be sold to any Multinational Corporations. Ganga is revered as a mother (Ganga Maa) and prayed to, and on its banks important ceremonies starting from birth till death are performed (according to Hindu religious practices). We will never allow our mother or its water to be sold to Suez-Degrémont or any other corporations.

The sacred waters of the Ganga cannot be the property of anyone individual or a company. Our mother Ganga is not for Sale. We boycott the commodification and privatisation of the Ganga and any other water resources.

We pledge to conserve and judiciously use our regional water resources to save our environment and ecology, so that we would gift our coming generation a clean and beautiful environment as well as safeguard their right to water resources.

We pledge and declare that the local community will have the right over the local water resources. It is the duty of the local community to conserve and sensibly utilise their resources. Anyone from outside the community whether an individual, an organisation or a corporation have to take permission of the Gram Sabha for utilising these resources.

The river Ganga was brought upon the face of earth by Bhagirath through his yagna (prayers) to sustain the existence of life on Earth. The Ganga is now intrinsic to our culture and a part of our heritage and our civilisation. Our life and progress over the millennia has been dependent upon the sacred waters of Ganga. We will fight any multinational company trying to take away our rights to life by privatising Ganga waters.

The 'Water Liberation Movement' will continue till we liberate the sacred waters of Ganga from the clutches of corporations, like Suez-Ondeo Degrémont.

Sacred waters carry us beyond the marketplace into a world charged with myth and stories, beliefs and devotion, culture and celebration. This is the world that enables us to save and share water, and convert scarcity into abundance. We are all Sagar's children, thirsting for waters that liberate and give us life—organically and spiritually. The struggle over the kumbh, between gods and demons, between those who protect and those who destroy, between those who nurture and those who exploit, is ongoing. Each of us has a role in shaping the creation story of the future. Each of us is responsible for the kumbh—the sacred water pot. This perennial creation story of which we are a part is the celebration at the Kumbh Mela where more than 30 million are gathered in Allahabad, recently renamed as Prayagraj, as I write these reflections. The Chipko poet, Ghanshyam Shailani, had called the Kumbh Mela the biggest party on earth, for which no one sends an invitation. The dedication and love for Ganga Ma is the call to which pilgrims have responded over centuries.

The movement to Save the Ganga and its *nirmal* (clean) and *aviral* (uninterrupted) flow is not just a movement to save a river. It is a movement to save India's troubled soul, polluted and stifled by crass consumerism and greed, disconnected from its ecological and cultural foundations. Our movement is based on the acknowledgement of the sanctity and sovereignty of the river Ganga. India's ecological civilisation lives in and through Ganga Ma.

If the Ganga lives, India lives. If the Ganga dies, India dies.

An island in an archipelago drained of time
Eimear Martin

I am Ganga
Snow from the mountains
The keeper of water
I am the plains
I am the foothills
I carry the wishes of my streams
To the sea
–Arvind Krishna Mehrotra, from *Songs of the Ganga*

Son of man,
You cannot say, or guess, for you know only
A heap of broken images, where the sun beats,
And the dead tree gives no shelter, the cricket no relief,
And the dry stone no sound of water. Only
There is shadow under this red rock,
(Come in under the shadow of this red rock),
And I will show you something different from either
Your shadow at morning striding behind you
Or your shadow at evening rising to meet you;
I will show you fear in a handful of dust.
–T.S. Eliot, from *The Waste Land*

I
Portrait of a river

Over a ten-year period starting in 2008, Giulio Di Sturco followed the entire 2,500 km course of the river Ganges downstream: from its source as snow in the Himalayan glaciers, to the Bay of Bengal where it empties into the Indian Ocean.

More than mere bodies of water, rivers are considered in many countries to hail from divine origins, and for Hindus the Ganges is the fulcrum of spirituality. Known as Ganga Ma (Mother Ganges), it is venerated as the physical manifestation of a goddess and extolled as a purifier of sins. Along its banks stand many of India's holy sites, places where bathing, purification ceremonies, and other traditional Hindu customs take place, such as entrusting the dead to the sacred river. Ironically, given its status, today the river is one of the most polluted in the world. India's hallowed artery has seen its water levels shrink and turn toxic, endangering the livelihoods of over 400 million people who depend on it for their sustenance, decimating countless species, and spoiling essential natural resources.

For the series Ganga Ma, Giulio Di Sturco turns his lens upon the ailing river. His photographs seldom depict more than two figures at a time, and when humans are present, they are preoccupied and rarely face the camera. People are secondary here, their lives complexly entwined with the waterway that sustains, sanctifies, and poisons them. The result is a portrait of the Ganges, one that compels us to reflect on the momentous impact of climate change, and the legacy of intensive agricultural production, industrialisation, and urbanisation along its banks.

In contrast to the sensory onslaught typical of the myriad exoticising images used to 'sell' India—bustling bazaars in kaleidoscopic hues, vertiginous throngs congregating on embankments—Di Sturco offers a perspective of quietude and restraint. Landscapes are barren, desolate, and strangely depopulated, a mood further enhanced by the use of startlingly simple compositions and desaturated colours. Here and there, man-made artefacts puncture the otherwise delicate tonal harmonies: a red sari blowing in the wind, a bright blue fishing net, a plastic sandal on the dusty ground.

In 2017, the High Court of the Indian state of Uttarakhand ruled that the Ganges and its main tributary, the Yamuna, should be granted the same rights as individuals. The law was overruled by the Supreme Court, who declared it legally unsustainable, but it nevertheless constituted a landmark in redefining the relationship between human and non-human entities. Di Sturco treats the Ganges as a character in its own right, a living entity with its own consciousness, voice, and agency. The river also provides the narrative and flow for this book, snaking through the landscape and taking us along on its course, enabling us to see the clusters of activity on its banks, as we might take in a landscape through the window of a moving train.

Ganga Ma was shot with a mixture of digital and analogue film. Di Sturco explains that the use of a medium-format analogue camera allowed him to slow things down, bringing him closer to his subjects, and enabling a high level of detail and colour accuracy. The resulting images may be seen as an aesthetic, painterly response to the specific ecological and atmospheric conditions of the Ganges, combined with aspects of the observational detachment familiar to documentary photography. In contrast to the detailed focus that marks many of the photographs in this series, there are a limited number of panoramic views, depicting bridges, or illegal sand mining. Here, the lofty perspective and use of a distant vantage point evoke the tradition of epic landscape painting. Listen, and other historical echoes can also be heard. An image of a couple with their backs to the camera, for instance, recalls the work of Caspar David Friedrich, whose paintings of sublime landscapes placed humans before vast and troubled expanses of land and sea, and who made use of a pictorial device known as *Rückenfigur*, in which the figure is shown from behind. The couple in Di Sturco's photograph stand facing the desolated riverbed in Bangladesh, where in place of water there are mounds of silt.

Di Sturco's photographs problematise the historical associations of 'the sublime.' In his treatise, *A Philosophical Enquiry into the Origin of Our*

Ideas of the Sublime and Beautiful (1757), Edmund Burke described the sublime as overwhelming and terrifying, yet '...delightful when we have an idea of pain and danger, without being actually in such circumstances...' *Ganga Ma* departs from the romantic tendency to view nature as an all-powerful force, something to be experienced vicariously and from a position of safety. Instead, the photographs in this series draw our attention to devastatingly real examples of environmental destruction, in which humans are participants and not spectators.

Di Sturco's choice of this most sacred and revered river as a subject speaks to the magnitude of environmental crisis in the era of the Anthropocene: a crisis that requires, in response, nothing less than a complete overhaul of the way we envision the relationship between people and the environment; the recalibration of the lens through which we perceive our place and agency in the world; and the granting of natural phenomena the status of living entity.

II
An aesthetics of pollution

Several images in *Ganga Ma* depict scenes of Hindu devotees preparing to bathe in the holy water of the Ganges during the Kumbh Mela in Allahabad. The world's largest mass religious pilgrimage, the Kumbh Mela takes place once every twelve years in this city and attracts tens of millions of pilgrims. Untreated sewage, industrial waste from neighbouring factories, agricultural runoffs, human remains from funeral pyres, and animal carcasses, make bathing risky. The river's poor health is compounded by a lack of infrastructure. The festival, which claims more visitors than the population of Scandinavia, has no effective clean-up policy: in their wake, pilgrims leave piles of garbage and human waste, which is at best disposed of by burning.

The photographs in *Ganga Ma* range from the banal to the quasi-surreal. As if to highlight the river's man-made infirmity, Di Sturco has adopted a striking aesthetic tactic: presenting images that at first glance appear beautiful and poetic, before revealing their true nature. A photograph of a man crossing the river on foot, for instance, looks like a graceful portrait of traditional rural life. Upon closer inspection, however, you will discover that the path he stands on is a submerged bridge made of waste. In one of the most striking and surreal images in the series, what looks like a lone iceberg floats along the river, adorned with bright garlands of orange and yellow marigold flowers. Look again, and the 'ice' reveals itself as chemical foam discharged by factories along the Yamuna river. Again, in the close-up photograph of the same phenomenon, a worker attempts to disperse the chemical foam-bergs with a hand-held hose, a Sisyphean task that seems doomed to failure.

The poetics of pollution is a theme many photographers have taken up. Notable among them is Edward Burtynsky, whose exploration of the transformative effects of industrialisation on the natural environment has been described as an expression of the 'toxic sublime.' Characterised by colossal, panoramic vistas that turn the landscape into macroscopic, highly formal patterns, Burtynsky's photographs re-imagine the sublime in a lexicon of environmental tragedy. Some of Di Sturco's images share an affinity with this approach–the majestic view of a bridge on the border of India and Bangladesh, for example, where the river is dry, owing to the closure of the Farakka Barrage. Unlike Burtynsky, however, Di Sturco also allows us to witness the effects of industrialisation up close, from the perspective of the river and its banks, and the results are both disquieting and beguiling. In a photograph taken on the outskirts of Kolkata, a lone, majestic-looking tree is depicted against a backdrop of electrical pylons and cabling. The pale, uneven terrain from which it appears to grow is made of mounds of leather off-cuts: the refuse from tanneries along the banks of the river.

At times, the images in *Ganga Ma* veer towards abstraction, drawing upon the environmental conditions to create subtle layers and gradations of colour, depth, and light. Such is the case with the first photograph included in this book, a dusty-pink colourfield in which a sinewy strip of land seems to merge with the sky and river, disappearing into infinite horizons. Indeed, light quality is crucial to Di Sturco's particular aesthetic of pollution. Shot primarily in the morning and evening, when light is at its softest, the images in *Ganga Ma* are suffused with a warm sand-colour, conveying the impression of parched land. Throughout the photographic process, there is no attempt to privilege either foreground or background, allowing light and tone to wash over the images without hierarchy. In this way, Di Sturco places subject and landscape on equal footing: a formal manifestation of an environmental world-view.

If each country has its own quality of light, *Ganga Ma* is suffused with a kind specific to South Asia: produced by the commingling of morning dew and sunlight, and compounded by widespread air pollution. In India, air pollution has reached such levels that the autumn has been named 'pollution season,' a time of the year when slower winds and cooler temperatures result in the blanketing of entire cities in a thick haze, causing major health issues among their populations. 'Haze' is an atmospheric phenomenon: a combination of dust, smoke, and other dry particulates that obscure the sun, scattering its light through a mass of airborne particles, subduing colours and inducing a loss of contrast. Because of the prevalent haze along the Ganges, the sun is never visible in *Ganga Ma*, and as a result, the pictures appear eerie and ethereal, an atmosphere conjured by meteorological means. In one carefully composed image, the photographer captures a cloud of pollution as it descends upon a man standing on the river's edge, engulfing him in a spectral veil.

Di Sturco's photographs belong to a genealogy of artists working with the formal properties of industrialisation and the aesthetic register of haze. They call to mind the early paintings of James Abbott McNeill Whistler, and the French Impressionists, who turned their attention to pollution in the West in the 1870s, seeking beauty in modern industry—producing work that could arguably be viewed as an 'environmental avant-garde.' The impressionists were interested in capturing the unique light effects and atmospheric conditions of the smog-filled cities they painted, most notably nineteenth century London which was colloquially known as 'The Big Smoke,' and where airborne pollution (as well as water pollution) was responsible for a great number of deaths. In Monet's painting *The Thames below Westminster* (c. 1871), a jetty casts sharp black shadows in the foreground, creating a stark contrast with Westminster and Big Ben, which are reduced to a faint blur by the murky air. A similar composition and contrast can be seen in Di Sturco's photograph of boats and barges, clearly visible against the barely discernible backdrop of enormous industrial chimneys billowing out smoke. Just as a rural pathway reveals itself to be submerged waste, or an iceberg chemical foam, here the veils of haze require closer, slower attention—in order that we might see what is hidden from view and consider the means by which it is hidden; in order that we might apprehend the strange and foreboding aesthetic register of our times.

III
The future is already here, it just isn't evenly distributed

In science fiction author J.G. Ballard's novel *The Drought* (1965) set in a parched future world decimated by pollution, the protagonist describes the impact of the loss of water, 'this great moderator,' which connects all things living and inanimate. The environmental conditions are threatening to indiscriminately reduce people and objects, he says, to islands 'in an archipelago drained of time.' Ballard innovated a form of writing known as 'speculative fiction,' using familiar characteristics from the present to describe a possible—and disastrous—near future. The perils of unchecked agriculture and industry have already irrevocably transformed and re-shaped our landscapes—transformations with grave consequences for the years ahead. It could be argued that Di Sturco's atmospheric body of work enacts a form of 'speculative photography': suggesting a not-so-distant future by showing us its seeds in the present day, and in the process allowing us to perceive a toxic, post-apocalyptic world.

The characteristic stillness of Di Sturco's images gives the impression that time as we know it has ceased to function. The usual visual clues that might help to locate the viewer are abstracted by the atmospheric haze, which makes objects and people appear to float in an uncertain chronology. The ruins of both destroyed and unrealised architectures, visible amidst *Ganga Ma*'s dystopian landscape, add to the temporal disorientation. Parts of an unfinished bridge, for example, are shown next to a makeshift outdoor laundry, and scenes of temporary camps, perhaps home to climate refugees, hint at the precarious forms of living that are becoming increasingly common. In certain photographs, landscapes appear as if only recently abandoned in the wake of an unspecified incident: empty leisure structures by the sea are left with only scaffolding; a picnic table with bright red plastic chairs propped up against it bears the unfinished remains of a meal.

Science fiction writer William Gibson famously said, 'The future is already here, it's just not very evenly distributed.' In other words, and as the photographs in *Ganga Ma* suggest, the building blocks of the future are already contained in the present. For now, they effect some people more than others, those exposed to the vagaries of climate change are often globally among the poorest, but it is only a matter of time until they multiply and become the 'new normal.' Owing to drastic disparities in wealth, natural resources, power, health, mobility, and access to technology, the inequalities of distribution will continue to widen if left unchecked–to devastating effect.

Ganga Ma began as a long-term documentary project, conceived of as a way to bear witness to an unfolding ecological disaster. In the process of making it, Di Sturco's focus shifted towards the creation of a visual language capable of responding to the changes already wrought upon the Ganges, and probing the landscape for signs of what is yet to come. Through veils of haze, these photographs explore an uncertain, precarious, and inhospitable future, which for many has already come to pass.

Acknowledgements

Thank you to everyone who made *Ganga Ma* possible.
All images were taken between 2008-2017 in India and Bangladesh.

Special thanks to:
Silvia, without whom nothing would be possible, Annalisa for giving new life to this body of work, Paolo for the delicate and incisive attention he brought to my images.
Ravi for being with me every step of the way and for his uncanny flair in finding the perfect spot.
Renata for believing in the project since the beginning, Matteo for his continued input and advice.
Vandana for her powerful text to accompany my photographs.
Stuart, Claudia and the GOST team.
And a very special thank you to Eimear for her words and for encouraging me to find a new visual language.
This book is for my family Anna, Carlo, Marcella and Maya.

First published in 2019 by
GOST Books
8a West Smithfield
London EC1A 9JR, UK
info@gostbooks.com
gostbooks.com

Photo Editing Consultant: Annalisa D'Angelo

Edited and designed by GOST:
Katie Clifford, Gemma Gerhard,
Allon Kaye, Claudia Paladini

Printed in Italy by EBS.

British Library cataloguing-in-publication data. A catalogue record of this book is available from the British Library.

ISBN 978-1-910401-28-6